Short Stories in English for Upper Intermediate Learners

Short Stories in English for Upper Intermediate Learners

Speed Up Your Language Acquisition With 20 Captivating Short Narrations

Acquire a Lot

San Rafael, California, USA

Copyright ©2023 Acquire a Lot. All rights reserved, include the rights of reproduction in whole or in part in any form. All wrongs avenged. No portion of this book may be reproduced in any form without permission from the publisher, except for the activities section.

Every effort has been made by the authors and publishing house to ensure that the information contained in this book was correct as of press time. The authors and publishing house hereby disclaim and do not assume liability for any injury, loss, damage, or disruption caused by errors or omissions, regardless of whether any errors or omissions result from negligence, accident, or any other cause. Readers are encouraged to verify any information contained in this book prior to taking any action on the information.

For rights, permissions or more information about this book please contact:

sergio@acquirealot.com

www.acquirealot.com

The characters and events portrayed in this book are fictitious. Any similarity to real persons, living or dead, is coincidental and not intended by the author.

ISBN-13: 9798379318925

Cover design by Sro

Printed in the United States of America

Dedicado a los estudiantes de idiomas al rededor del mundo. Escucha y escucharás.

Table of Contents

INTRODUCTION 1

An Adventure in Teotihuacan 4

The Arcade 10

The Beautiful Game 16

The Colorful Water 22

Camp Green Lake 29

Camping 34

Doctor Visit 40

Grandma's Parakeet 46

Island Experience 52

Kim's Beach 58

Lost in New York 64

Movie Night 70

Mummy Museum 77
My Day at the Farm 83
Rainbow Land.. 90
The Recital 96
Shooting Stars 102
Stone Soup 108
The Two Ollies...114
Zookeeping 120
Answers 126
About the Author 128
A special request..128
Books in this Series....................................129
Books By This Author 130

INTRODUCTION

Welcome to our upper-intermediate book of short stories for the acquisition of the English language. Whether you have started here with this book or worked your way through our previous editions, we hope this book will serve you well in your journey to fluency in English.

The main goal with this volume is to help you with the acquisition of more complex language elements such as conjunctions, abbreviations and colloquialisms.

The second goal of this book is to help you acquire a broader grasp of the English language and expand your vocabulary. This book is a series of short stories, each designed to challenge your understanding of English grammar and language in general. The stories include characters that will be using the more advanced language tools such as conjunctions, abbreviations and colloquialisms referenced earlier. The aim is to introduce more casual modes of speech that the learner may not be used to and include systems that may not be grammatically correct but are indeed used in standard English conversation.

The intent behind these stories is to challenge you more than the content of our last volume, each story contains language quirks that you may be unfamiliar with in the hopes that this will aid in increasing your comprehension and acquisition of these articles. If you feel challenged by these stories don't worry, that's the point! A key aspect of language acquisition, especially within the method of the natural approach that this book endorses, is challenge while in a relaxing environment. When you find yourself challenged you mentally focus. This combined with the lack of pressure a casual storytelling environment creates will aid you in vocabulary retention. This results in much faster and more effective than if you were continuing to learn English at a level that does not fully engage you mentally.

Finally each story will provide both a VOCABULARY and summary to aid your learning along with a small test to help you test your level of comprehension. Using these tools will help you learn some of the more complex words in the stories along with adding further comprehension to help you add these words to your everyday vocabulary. If you find these stories effective a fantastic next step would be to practice reading them aloud with a friend or family member, vocalizing helps aid vocabulary retention and will result in further linguistic development. Attempting to use some of the more casual language structures or discussing them with others will also be fantastic aid in your language journey. Once again thank you for your selection of this book for your language journey and we hope it serves you well.

4

An Adventure in Teotihuacan

Edward had never been to the ancient city before and as the truck drove closer to its final destination he could feel his body almost **vibrate** with excitement. His parents had had a handful keeping their boy occupied over the school holidays and almost jumped at the chance to send them to his uncle for the weekend. Edward knew his uncle lived in a small suburb only 20 minutes from the park where Teotihuacan was and had begged his uncle over the phone to take him to the city until he finally relented. Though he knew his uncle loved the **region**'s history and would have been eager to take him anyway.

So here he was, in the car with his uncle watching the road turn from highway to bumpy cobblestones as they reached Teotihuacan. They had gotten there early, eating a small breakfast of "huevos rancheros" before heading there, Edwards' aunt promising a delicious meal of Mole would be waiting for them on their return home. Edward wasn't an early riser usually but his uncle had warned him there would be little shade from the midday sun and wanted them to see as much as they could before they were overwhelmed by the heat and the crowds. It was already a warm day as his uncle parked the car, and as they paid the entrance fee Edward marveled at hot air balloons he could see rise in the distance thinking one day he would love to take one and see the temples from above.

Edward couldn't see much else yet, the street to the city was lined with stalls blocking his view, his uncle bought them both a large bottle of water and a snack before they continued. "Maybe next time we will get some Chaplains' nephew" said Edwards uncle winking at him, he knew Edward had a slight fear of bugs and the idea of grasshoppers grossed him out, no matter how much his uncle told him that they were delicious when had with a bit of chili, salt and lime.

"Do you know what the most common food of the Aztecs was?" his uncle continued. Edward thought hard. It had to be corn' he thought, everyone loves corn.

"Maize Uncle?" responded Edward, not too sure knowing his uncle loved a question that had a surprise answer.

"Good guess little Ed but not quite, our ancestors loved squash, a long time ago everything around us was a grand lake and they made great islands that floated in the water, we grew squash as it loved the wet soil." His uncle laughed before adding "We probably would have had to have taken a boat to get to the city, not my car."

Edward was fascinated, he looked around at the beautiful but dry land and tried to imagine the floating islands and canals that the ferrymen would have taken.

Edwards' uncle continued his personal tour, loving the chance to be a guide to his young nephew, showing him how Aztecs would use shallow reflective pools to track the movement of the stars and moon or once they finally reached the city proper the grand temples of the sun and moon. They were huge temples of stone, towering over the rest of the ancient city. Edward could barely believe the grand structures were real, impressed by his ancestors ability to construct such large structures, he was at a loss for words until his uncle interrupted the silence, eager to give his nephew another **factoid**.

"Do you remember your Grandma's nesting doll nephew? A doll within a doll, each one smaller than the last? These temples are like that, each one built on top of the previous one, the rulers of the city eager to show their glory and respect for the gods."

Edward felt awe, he could almost imagine when the city was still alive, the largest of its time like the Mexico City of today, filled with color, activity and people going about their lives in the shadow of these grand temples, if he had time travel he thought, he would most certainly go there to see the city in its prime.

Edwards's uncle had gone ahead, he could tell his uncle was excited to share more knowledge with him. His uncle placed his hands on his shoulders and gently guided him to the front of one of the smaller temple stairs, taking his place next to Edward he turned to him.

"You'll love this my nephew, one of the Aztecs most holy symbols was the Quetzal bird, their feathers are what make such grand headdresses for the high priests, but they lived far away from Teotihuacan, so our clever ancestors made the next best thing. Clap with me for a moment."

Edward's curiosity was spiked and he clapped with his uncle and was shocked it was almost as if the temples chirped back at him like a bird!

"The Aztecs were very smart as you can see, they built their cities perfectly in line with the sun and moon and even made them talk back!" his uncle laughed "every day we find more of the city in the hills, so much history for us to find, maybe you'll be an archeologist one day and find even more places like this doesn't that sound fun?" his Uncle asked.

Edward couldn't deny, he was in love with the city and wanted to find more, he knew he would love to **dedicate** himself to finding more of his countries past, it filled him with pride to see these amazing achievements but it was that time his stomach began to rumble, he was surprised it didn't make the temple Squawk again it was so loud.

His uncle heard and said to him "Perhaps you've had your fill of history for one day my nephew, maybe it's time we had our fill of mole" and they both laughed, as much as Edward wanted to stay and see more a delicious lunch of his aunts home cooking was too good to pass up, with his uncle they began to walk back to the car but Edward knew it would not be the last time he went to the wonderful city of Teotihuacan.

SUMMARY

Edward is spending the weekend at his Uncle and Aunts house outside Mexico City and is excited to go to the nearby archeological site Teotihuacan. In the morning Edward travels with his uncle to the ancient city who proceeds to give him a small tour of the various locations. After being amazed by the advanced architecture of the city the two begin to make their way home for lunch. Edward resolving to become an archeologist because of the interesting things he has seen in Teotihuacan.

Edward está pasando el fin de semana en la casa de sus tíos en las afueras de la Ciudad de México y está emocionado de ir al sitio arqueológico cercano de Teotihuacan. Por la mañana, Edward viaja con su tío a la ciudad antigua, en donde procede a darle un pequeño recorrido por los distintos lugares. Después de estar asombrados por la arquitectura avanzada de la ciudad, los dos comienzan a regresar a casa para almorzar. Edward decide convertirse en arqueólogo debido a las cosas interesantes que ha visto en Teotihuacan.

VOCABULARY

Vibrate: Moverse hacia adelante y hacia atrás o hacia arriba y hacia abajo rápida y repetidamente.

Region: Una gran área o rango de algo especificado.

Marvelled: El sentimiento de asombro; asombro.

Dedicate: Dedicar, dedicación.

Factoid: Un hecho o dato relevante.

QUESTIONS

1. What sound does the temple echo sound like?

A) A crash.

B) A bark.

C) A Squawk.

D) A moo.

E) It doesn't make a sound.

2. What meal do Edward and his uncle go home to?

A) Mole.

B) Stew.

C) Sandwiches.

D) Salsa.

E) Soup.

3. What fear does Edward have?

A) Birds.

B) Dogs.

C) Bugs.

D) Snakes.

E) Heights.

4. What food does Edward guess is the Aztecs favorite?

A) Squash.

B) Corn.

C) Beans.

D) Cheese.

E) Tortillas.

5. What is in the sky near the temples?

A) Birds.

B) Planes.

C) Clouds.

D) Air Balloons.

E) Helicopters.

The Arcade

Randy's fifteenth birthday was a special one. He and his friends had decided to go to the **arcade** that had just opened up in their neighborhood. The Belleview Arcade was an arcade with a huge video game area in the center, a small pinball arcade on one side and food court on another with an ice-cream shop and a burger stall etc. There was also a large indoor trampoline room! A lot of kids would go there to play video games. Randy's friends were the only kids in his grade who didn't play games, or at least they weren't playing video-games. His friends were always playing games on the football field, handball court or playground. When Randy first saw the Belleview Arcade, he thought it looked very impressive. He was very impressed with how it could hold all that arcade game stuff he thought, as well as the **trinket** store where he was hoping to cash his tickets for a prize. He was so excited that he almost forgot to exchange his change for tokens so he could play the machines he heard in the distance, their electronic beeps and music calling to him from the entrance.

Once Randy and his friends had paid their fee and exchanged their pocket money for tokens they rushed inside to find the games they had been waiting for. They found a game called "wacky racers", a large multiplayer racing game and they all played for almost an hour. After they played a few rounds, they decided that they would play another game that was much more difficult, but also very popular. That game was called 'Invaders From Space', they each took turns defending earth from endless waves of aliens, tilting the joystick back and forth attempting to dodge alien lasers while protecting their base. Randy could almost hear the **sizzle** of the lasers rush past him as he played, he was in the zone and even got into the high scores! He won a lot more than he lost, so his score was high enough to get a free game for the next day. It was now time to move on though, all of his friends were eager to try the trampoline room, where they could jump and play together. So Randy, with his best friend Paul, decided they should all go. Before they left, Randy asked his friend to take his picture with the Invaders From Space machine, the flash of his friend's camera blinded his eyes but he didn't mind, rubbing them and seeing stars until his sight returned.

The Trampoline room was huge Randy had never seen anything like it, the walls were covered in rubber and the floor was covered in all sorts of bouncy surfaces. They were named all sorts of strange things: tramps, tronks, tandems, bouncers, jumpers and trilobites. Some of them were so large they were able to bounce people to the ceiling, some were even able to bounce from one side of the room to another. The birthday group rushed into the room and began to play, each of them having a great time. Some of Randy's friends were helping the others jump even higher, almost reaching the padded roof. 'People must hit their heads occasionally.' Thought Randy as he observed his friends, but he was more focused on the trampoline known as 'The Launchpad', a trampoline placed at an angle so when you jumped off the platform above it, it would launch you across the room and over a pit filled with foam. Randy felt the rush of excitement rise as he leap from the platform onto the trampoline below, he felt himself sink into the elastic canvas of the trampoline before being rocketed forward, his vision a jumble of roof and foam pit as he tumbled through the air before landing without grace into the center of the pit. He laughed loudly, he had never had such fun, he had loved the arcade games but had never experienced anything like this. He and his friends enjoyed the rest of the day at the Trampoline area, only occasionally **venturing** out for snacks from the ice cream and burger bars or to collect more tickets from the arcade machines.

The time had come though, after a few hours that the arcade was about to close. Randy and his friends heard the announcement of the loudspeakers and began to get ready to leave. Their parents would be expecting them home soon or be coming to pick them up outside. Randy checked his pockets for his tickets but was met with nothing but lint, he groaned realizing his tickets must have fallen out as he used the launchpad trampoline. He considered trying to find them but knew he'd never find them in time in the gigantic foam pit. He prepared to leave full of sadness that he would not be getting any prizes today, a sad end to an otherwise perfect birthday party.

Randy's friends could see his disappointment and decided together that they would help save his birthday, pooling their tickets together while Randy made his way to the entrance they bought an action figure and a small fortune's worth of candy. Randy was so caught up in his lost tickets that he was even more taken aback and delighted when his friends presented him their gift, he was overcome by their **generosity** and hugged each of his friends, thanking them endlessly. As the young boys got ready to leave Randy made sure to share out an equal share of the candy to everyone in the group to make sure no one was left out. He had learned that the present he valued most was the kindness and generosity of his friends and wanted to continue their example and return it in kind. All the children left the Arcade that day full of joy, happy knowing that all their friends were good, kind and knew the value of friendship.

SUMMARY

Randy and his friends gather for his birthday, heading to the new local arcade. Randy and his friends enjoy various arcade video games and food before finding the trampoline section. The boys quickly find that this is their favorite place in the arcade and spend most of their time there enjoying the various trampolines till closing time. Once closing arrives the friends once again gather to leave but Randy has found that he has lost his tokens for prizes, making him very sad. His friends decide to surprise him by pooling their tickets together to get him a prize and a large amount of candy. Randy is so happy and taken by this display of friendship that he shares the candy out of gratitude before the children leave.

Randy y sus amigos se reúnen por su cumpleaños y se dirigen a la nueva sala de juegos local. Ellos disfrutan de varios videojuegos arcade y comida antes de encontrar la sección de trampolines. Los chicos descubren rápidamente que este es su lugar favorito en la sala de juegos y pasan la mayor parte del tiempo allí disfrutando de los diversos trampolines hasta la hora del cierre. Una vez que llega el cierre, los amigos se reúnen una vez más para irse, pero Randy descubre que ha perdido sus fichas de premios, lo que lo entristece mucho. Sus amigos deciden sorprenderlo juntando sus boletos para conseguirle un premio y una gran cantidad de dulces. Randy está tan feliz y cautivado por esta muestra de amistad que comparte los dulces en agradecimiento antes de que los niños se vayan.

VOCABULARY

Arcade: Un establecimiento, área pública, etc., que contiene juegos de tipo mecánico y electrónico, como pinball y videojuegos, que puede jugar un cliente por una tarifa.

Trinket: Un pequeño adorno, pieza de joyería, etc., generalmente de poco valor.

Sizzle: Hacer un sonido de silbido, como al freír o quemar.

Venturing: Salir.

Generosity: Generosidad.

QUESTIONS

1. What is the main character's name?

A) Randy.

B) Brandy.

C) Steve.

D) Gary.

E) Jim.

2. Which of these ISN'T a trampoline that the boys see?

A) Tramps.

B) Tronks.

C) Tandems.

D) Bounder.

E) Bouncers.

3. What does Randy give his friends?

A) Treats.

B) Candy.

C) Toys.

D) Tickets.

E) Trinkets.

4. What is the second game the boys play?

A) Invaders From Space.

B) Wacky Racers.

C) Trampoline Land.

D) Hockey.

E) Pinball.

5. What game did the boys like to play at school?

A) Volleyball.

B) Netball.

C) Kickball.

D) Baseball.

E) Handball.

The Beautiful Game

Terry had been soccer mad ever since he got his own ball for his fifth birthday. He terrorized his household by dribbling the ball wherever he went, imagining his brothers and sisters moving about the house were defenders he was **dodging** and weaving around before lining up his own perfect goal. More often than not he would be shooed out of the house to the backyard by his mother, desperate to keep him from knocking over another vase or pot plant. It continued like this for another seven years until finally Terry had achieved his dream: A spot on his school's soccer team 'The Wolverines'.

But Terry had a secret, as much as his moves on the field impressed his teammates, he could never tell them how he'd acquired such perfect skills in maneuvering around his opponents on the pitch. It all began two years ago when Terry went with his older sister Maria to her dance class, he had protested greatly but it'd be an hour before anyone could pick them up to go home and their mother Gabriella knew all too well that Terry had a habit of getting into **mischief** while alone. While he was initially upset to see something as boring as ballroom dance, he was soon fascinated as he watched the dancers move with **fluidity** and grace, moving around each other in coordinated skill. He knew what he had to do: bring the art of dance to soccer. It had been surprisingly easy to convince his sister to let him join in, the class enjoyed such a young boy eager to learn and he quickly became something of a mascot to the older dancers, often being referred to as 'the little wind' for his smaller size and fluid movements.

Ever since that day his rise to the top of his local soccer pitch had seemed all but guaranteed, every time he danced around another defender, already repositioning to shoot the perfect goal he recalled his dance training of spins and **pirouettes**, Maria on the sidelines always giving support to her little brother but never revealing his secret. Terry had adored the last two years his dancing had even taken him to some local competitions! He felt like his skills on the pitch increased every day even more than his dancing and while he had a few close calls with friends wondering where he disappeared to twice a week, he had so far been able to keep his two lives separate with minimal drama, but that was all to change on the day of the regional intermediate soccer championship.

It was an unusually humid summer day, every team was struggling with the heat and playing game after game, even Terry's dance improved conditioning was starting to suffer. It took all his focus to **maintain** the pressure and dazzle his opponents with his artful foot work, but the day had so far been a success. The Wolverines found victory over the rival school's teams 'The Jaguars' and 'The Bulls' which brought them to the semi-finals, a first for the team in almost four years! Terry took to the pitch, taking his role on the left flank adjacent to his friend Patel who when it came to Soccer was a natural wingman, always knowing just when to offer Terry the ball so he could work his magic. But something was off, the opposing team 'The Bulldogs' took to the field and Terry couldn't shake the feeling he knew his counterpart from the opposite team, a girl his age with the same focus and determination he saw in himself. Who was this girl and why did Terry feel like he had seen her before?

The game began and Terry's confusion only grew, with every trick he tried the mystery girl had a response and without either team's star player able to make a break the game ground on as a zero-point tie well into the second half. Terry was shaken, who was this mysterious girl who could predict his every move? Finally in the last five minutes of the game the unthinkable happened, Terry struck out to his left to block his counterpart and watched her dance fluidly around his opposite side, all he could do was watch as the girl breezed past his fellow teammates and scored the first goal of the game, there was nothing more to do, try as he might there wasn't enough time and the game ended in favor of 'The Bulldogs'.

The loss stung as it took The Wolverines out of the final round, but the team were good sportsmen one and all and lined up for the **customary** post game handshake. But Terry had to know as he came up to his rival for the handshake he asked, "Where do I know you from, how did you beat me?"

"You don't recognize me Terry? We met a few months ago at the last Ballroom dance meet." the girl replied not realizing the secret she had revealed in front of Terry's whole team. The color drained from Terry's face; his pulse quickened as he looked around at the shocked faces of his team around him.

"Is that where you've been going every week Terry?" said Patel "we thought it was some sort of secret Soccer camp with how good you are." He continued but already Terry was turning away, he had to get off the pitch so his friends wouldn't see his cheeks flush red from embarrassment.

'I'll never live this down' he thought 'I'll be the laughingstock of the whole team'.

Terry had Maria take him home immediately and refused to leave his room for the rest of the weekend, not wanting to see his friends till Monday, hoping the shock would die down by then. School was a close call, but he made himself scarce between classes and managed to get through the day with little hassle. It wasn't till later in the day he would see his friends in the last place he would have expected. Maria had picked him up from school and they made their way to dance practice and what Terry saw there shocked him. Patel was there along with several other members of his team!

"Patel, what are you all doing here?" he asked, confused and surprised to see them all at his secret class. "Well we asked around Terry, now that we know you dance we figured if one of us learning to dance can take us all the way to the soccer finals imagine if all of us did, we'd be unstoppable!" Patel replied. Terry could feel the tension leaving his body and he laughed, he never had anything to worry about because his friends wanted to be as good as he was! Terry was overjoyed he could now openly share his second passion with his friends and next year if they worked hard they might finally take the championship.

"Let me show you how to warm up and then some of my favorite moves" Terry said joining his friends, it was going to be a good year.

SUMMARY

Terry is an avid football player ever since he found a passion for it at a young age. Terry is experiencing much success on his school's football team but he is hiding a secret, the reason he's so graceful and fluid on the field is because he has been taking secret dance lessons and using the skills he's learned on the football field. Terry has managed to keep his secret successfully up until now when, after being defeated by a similarly skilled player she unknowingly reveals his secret to his team. Upset and embarrassed that his team now know his secret he avoids them all till his next dance class where he finds some of his friends waiting. They explain that they too want to learn dancing in the hopes that they may become as skilled as him. Terry is happy his friends don't find his secret embarrassing and agrees to help them learn.

Terry es un ávido jugador de fútbol, desde que encontró la pasión por él fútbol a una edad temprana. Terry está teniendo mucho éxito en el equipo de fútbol de su escuela, pero esconde un secreto, la razón por la que es tan elegante y fluido en el campo es porque ha estado tomando lecciones secretas de baile y usando las habilidades que aprendió en el campo de fútbol. Terry ha logrado mantener su secreto con éxito hasta ahora, cuando, después de ser derrotado por un jugador con habilidades similares, sin saberlo, revela su secreto a su equipo. Molesto y avergonzado porque su equipo ahora sabe su secreto, los evita a todos hasta su próxima clase de baile, donde encuentra a algunos de sus amigos esperando. Explican que ellos también quieren aprender a bailar con la esperanza de llegar a ser tan hábiles como él. Terry está feliz de que sus amigos no encuentren su secreto vergonzoso y accede a ayudarlos a aprender.

VOCABULARY

Dodging: Moverse a un lado o cambiar de posición repentinamente.

Mischief: Conducta o actividad que juguetonamente causa molestias menores.

Fluidity: Fluidez.

Pirouettes: Piruetas, giro sobre un pie o sobre las puntas de los dedos.

Customary: Según o dependiendo de la costumbre.

QUESTIONS

1. Who Is the main character's friend?
A) Terry.
B) Maria.
C) Patel.
D) Marty.
E) Peter.

2. What kind of dancing does Terry learn?
A) Disco.
B) Ballroom.
C) Salsa.
D) Breakdancing.
E) Ballet.

3. When does Terry get his first football?
A) At 5.
B) At 6.
C) At 4.
D) At 7.
E) At 8.

4. What is Terrys football team name?
A) The Bulldogs.
B) The Bulls.
C) The Wolverines.
D) The Badgers.
E) The Wolves.

5. How many years has Terry been practicing dance?
A) 2 Months.
B) 3 Years.
C) 3 Months.
D) 2 Years.
E) 1 Year.

The Colorful Water

If there was one thing Elouise knew Anthony loved it was the **Aquarium**, ever since his mother took him as a young boy he had been fascinated by the underwater world. That's why he was so **relentless** in getting his big sister to take him while they were both on their school holidays. It had been a battle, ever since Elouise had become a senior in high school Tony felt as though she didn't have much time for her little brother anymore.

"C'mon Elly we need to get there before the line gets too big!" Anthony exclaimed as he tugged on her sleeve pulling them across the parking lot.

"You know no one calls me Elly anymore it's 'Louise' and calm down Tony you'll pull my arm off! You're lucky I even agreed to bring you here." Elouise pulled her sleeve back, taking care to fix its cuff. "Anyway I don't know why you want to come here so much; it's just going to be a dark tunnel full of smelly fish." Elouise could see Anthony was shocked his sister would say such a thing about his favorite place.

"NOT TRUE!" he yelled "you're just saying that because you'll never come whenever me and mom go."

Anthony knew the situation was **dire** as they paid for entrance at the ticket booth, he had to show his sister the best part of the aquarium straight away if he was to make Elouise see that this place was as magical as he had said.

"This way Elly!" Anthony hollered as he ran ahead.

He ran past the exhibits of bleached whale bones and old arctic explorer equipment, already becoming lost in the crowd to Elouise.

"IT'S LOUISE TONY" an exasperated Elouise yelled back as she began to give chase, receiving a few concerned looks and dismissive 'tuts' as she pursued her brother through the aquarium crowd. Elouise was the bigger and faster of the two being seven years older than her little brother but that didn't count for much in the crowded aquarium **atrium**. Tony's smaller size and agility helped him slip between the groups of people milling around the exhibits where Elouise had to politely push past and apologize. Elouise had just enough time to see her little brother dart past the penguin enclosure and down a flight of stairs with the sign 'THE UNDERWATER EXPERIENCE' placed above it, she politely excused herself as she pushed between two groups of tourists staring at a large red replica of an arctic rover. Elouise reached the stairs and descended after her slippery little brother, determined to catch up to him.

Catching her breath at the bottom of the stairs Elouise had to take a moment to recover and as she did, she had to admit she was only half right so far about the aquarium. It was dark but not unpleasantly so, a soft blue light lit the path ahead **illuminating** the floor in a gentle glow. As her eyes adjusted, she could see something strange about the path ahead, was it moving? It was! The path itself moved at a leisurely pace like a flat escalator. Elouise gingerly stepped on and began moving forward, the aquarium seemed to be a long tunnel with the top half being a glass casing, giving an unprecedented view of the water and environment above her.

Elouise had a mission, she had to find that little brother of hers and give him a piece of her mind for running off like that when their mother had specifically said to look after him! She'd be grounded for the rest of the school holiday if their mother found out about this, how could tony be so selfish? But once again she had to admit the aquarium was very pretty and it didn't smell like fish. She found herself being distracted by the panoramic view of the tunnel, It had opened up to a wide view of an underwater kingdom. All around her was like a pastel dream of color, towers of coral reef shifting from a dusty red to sandy yellow and then to a jade blue, flanked on all sides by vibrant green seaweed that drifted lazily in the current, almost like it was waving. A movement just in the corner of Elouises eye caught her attention, hidden amongst the reef, nesting in one of the pale red rocks was… was it a water snake? No! Elouise realized it was an eel! Its long body slowly snaking out was much thicker than any snake she had ever seen, its soft texture, wide glassy eyes, bright yellow coloration and toothless smile reminded her more of a sock puppet than a snake. Elouise had to suppress a laugh as it looked at her, she almost wanted one for a pet.

It was hard not to be distracted by the magical colors on display in the aquarium, schools of fish swam past glittering from the light above like jewels. Flashes of light from azure blue scales dazzled Elouise's eyes like diamonds, she was in a natural kaleidoscope of color, the fish moving and forming patterns to some unknown purpose, long skinny green fish mingled with multicolored fish, striped like tigers it was like nothing she had ever seen before, she watched intently as they swam ahead. That was when Elouise saw something that caused her much concern, it was an intersection ahead! There was a new tunnel to the right and which way did Anthony go? she wondered. If she chose wrong, Anthony might get scared since he was alone for a while now, despite her annoyance Elouise loved her brother and wasn't pleased by the idea of him being alone and afraid. The path pulled her closer to the two tunnels intersection she soon had to make a choice but where? Hurriedly she looked for clues to where her brother had gone but he had left none. Elouise spied something curious though, between the two tunnels a Smack of jellyfish floated, Elouise remembered her brother telling her that the name of a herd of jellyfish was called a Smack, he'd giggled all day when he found out. The neon pink jelly bodies with limp electric blue tentacles floated in place but it seemed almost with purpose, Elouise thought she might be going crazy but could almost swear the tentacles were pointing ever so slightly to the right. Trusting her gut (and the Jellyfish) she stepped onto the new path and continued her journey, walking quickly now hoping to catch up with her little brother.

This path was a little shorter than the other; it seemed looping on itself quickly 'maybe it's like a rest stop' Elouise thought as she moved ahead and around the bend, what she saw took her breath away. The largest window in the aquarium so far. It was like a wall of color, the masses of fish swimming together in beautiful patterns, like a freeform rainbow. Elouise could not count all the colors on display. It was so beautiful she almost didn't notice the small boy staring at the window as well, it was her brother!

"Tony" she gasped running over as he turned to face her.

"Elly" cried Anthony, his smile wide. "I'm sorry I thought you were right behind me; I was just so excited to show you" he continued.

"It's okay Tony I'm just glad I found you, you can't go running off like that again!" Elouise wrapped her arms around Anthony in a big tight hug like she used to when they were younger. "But you're right this Aquarium is a lovely place."

Anthony broke into an even bigger smile. "I told you Elly, aren't you glad you came?"

"Yes, I am Tony but what did I say about calling me Elly?" She said, her voice returning to its usual big sister tone.

Anthony's face dropped slightly "ok Louise."

Elouise smiled and raised his chin with her hand "How about a deal, you can call me Elly all day as long as you don't tell mom I lost you."

With that they both broke out into laughter and spoke of what an adventure they'd had so far today.

"Ok Elly but I want to take you to see the sharks" Anthony said as the laughter faded

"I'd like that but you'll be staying with me the whole time little brother" Elouise said warmly as she took her little brother's hand in hers "why don't you show me the way?"

SUMMARY

Elouise takes her younger brother Anthony to the local aquarium. She has never gone as she has never been interested in the sea but her brother finds it fascinating. After a small argument Anthony rushes ahead in excitement and Elouise loses him in the crowd. During her search she sees a large amount of what the aquarium has to offer, becoming fascinated by the varied wildlife on display in their underwater habitats. Eventually Elouise finds her younger brother and they apologize for their argument. The story ends with Elouise learning to appreciate her brother's interests and willingly exploring the aquarium with him further.

Elouise lleva a su hermano menor Anthony al acuario local. Ella nunca ha ido porque nunca le ha interesado el mar, pero su hermano lo encuentra fascinante. Después de una pequeña discusión, Anthony se adelanta emocionado y Elouise lo pierde entre la multitud. Durante su búsqueda, ve una gran cantidad de lo que el acuario tiene para ofrecer, quedando fascinada por la variada vida silvestre que se exhibe en sus hábitats submarinos. Finalmente, Elouise encuentra a su hermano menor y se disculpan por su discusión. La historia termina con Elouise aprendiendo a apreciar los intereses de su hermano y voluntariamente explorando más el acuario con él.

VOCABULARY

Aquarium: Un edificio o institución en la que se observan peces u otros animales o plantas acuáticas para exhibición, estudio.

Relentless: Sin aflojar ni aflojar; manteniendo la velocidad.

Dire: Urgente; desesperado.

Atrium: Una sala o patio central en un edificio moderno, con salas o galerías que se abren, a menudo cubiertas de vidrio.

Illuminating: Dar luz.

QUESTIONS

1. What is Anthony's sister's name?

A) Ellen.

B) Elouise.

C) Louise.

D) Louie.

E) Tony.

2. Where are they going?

A) The Zoo.

B) The Museum.

C) The Ocean.

D) The Aquarium.

E) To School.

3. How much older is the sister compared to Anthony?

A) 6 Years.

B) 6 Months.

C) 7 Years.

D) 7 Months.

E) They are the same age.

4. What is a group of jellyfish called?

A) Smack.

B) Speck.

C) Smash.

D) School.

E) Swarm.

5. What color are the Jellyfish tentacles?

A) Red.

B) Pink.

C) Yellow.

D) Green.

E) Blue.

Camp Green Lake

If Gary had to say what his favorite place in the world was it would be Camp Green Lake. His parents had sent him here every summer for almost four years now and he was more excited than ever to go now, at fifteen he was finally old enough to take sailing lessons and go out on the lake with his friends. Watching his older brother Jake go out on the water last year filled him with envy, seeing the small sailing boat called a sunfish cut though the water in a zig zagging motion as it used the wind to move forward, he couldn't wait to feel the freedom of the open water and the cool spray of the water as his own boat cut through the lake. He had signed up first thing before even unpacking or greeting his friends, he would not be taking the chance that he wouldn't be in the class this year.

Camp life continued as normal, **orientation** and first dinner being a great time to reconnect with friends made last year, other campers talking about their favorite classes and which they signed up for first. His brother Jake had not taken sailing this year, preferring to focus on land activities, since last year he had joined an **outdoorsman** club and found a passion for archery and orienteering now considering himself an explorer of the woods around the lake, though he hoped he wouldn't run into any bears! Gary's camp buddy Hiro on the other hand had signed up for sailing but was even more excited for sports, he had practiced for soccer all year and was eager to make the team for the inter-camp competitions. That night it was hard for Gary to sleep, the day had been busy and exhausting, seeing old friends and organizing his camp calendar but the excitement of what tomorrow would bring was keeping him awake! He wasn't sure when he fell asleep but it couldn't have been for long and when he woke up at seven in the morning he felt like he had barely slept at all! **Groggy** but eager Gary brushed his teach showered and had breakfast with the other campers, all he could talk about as he had his meal of eggs and toast was the sailing he'd do that day, he was sure the other campers were already starting to get tired of hearing him talk about it but he couldn't help himself.

He was the first to the dock once breakfast had finished, beating even the instructors in his haste. It wasn't long before the other campers who had elected to sail had arrived and they began their first and most important lesson of all: safety. Each camper was taught how to properly affix a life vest, making sure it would be tight and keep their head above water in case they fell off the boat. Gary was a confident swimmer but the camp legend went that no one knew how deep the lake was so he was sure to listen closely, he'd hate to have to swim all the way back to shore if there was an emergency!

It wasn't long before the class tutors started pairing students off to work on attaching masts to the small **fiberglass** craft they would be training in, each boat large enough for two students and one instructor. The masts were light enough for two students to pick up, Gary and his partner Maury having no difficulty raising theirs and affixing it to the center of the boat. The next part of the lesson was to rig the sail, looping ropes through parts of the boat and sail to connect the two and help it steer before tying specific knots so they wouldn't lose it in a gust of wind. Gary and Maurice worked fast and the instructors were impressed by their good work, it wasn't long before the two were selected to sail, the instructor boarding their boat as they pushed off from the dock, tutoring them on how to steer with and against the wind, how to slow their boat and how to bring it into dock. Impressed by their skill the instructor brought them close to the dock before jumping off to teach others, leaving Gary and Maury alone to enjoy some time sailing while the others were trained.

Gary and Maury wondered how to use their time to themselves, Maury was **content** to just enjoy their time in the water and sun but Gary knew exactly what he wanted to do. Gary steered the boat along the long coast of the lake, sailing with the wind in his sails to where he could see all his other friends as they worked on their own favorite activity. Bringing the boat close to shore Gary and Maury could see the football fields as they traveled, waving they got Hiro's attention and cheered him on as they watched him score a goal. Next up they sailed close to the archery preserve, thankfully the targets faced the dense forest and not the water! Gary could see his brother draw an arrow before letting it fly towards the target, Gary was impressed with his accuracy and knew he would be an expert shot by the end of the summer.

It was getting close to the end of their time on the water and Gary slowly sailed him and Maury back along the way they came, crossing the boat back and forth like their instructor showed them so they could move against the wind. The instructor was waiting for them as they brought their craft to the dock, he complimented the teams skill, saying he'd like to see them prepare for the sailing competition against their rival camp this season. Gary and his new friend Maury were delighted, not only that but Gary was filled with a new passion to try his friends' sports as seeing them play had filled him with excitement. It was going to be a busy summer but that didn't bother Gary, he knew it was going to be one of the most exciting of his life.

SUMMARY

Gary is excited to go to summer camp, this will be the first year he will be old enough to take sailing lessons. Gary spends his first day with his friends, each of them discussing the activity they most look forward to. Gary's brother wants to learn archery while his friend Hiro wants to learn football. The next day Gary and his sailing partner Maury begin their lessons, their instructor is impressed with their progress and lets them sail unattended while he teaches the others. As Gary and Maury sail they watch Gary's friends perform the activities they enjoy and cheer them on from the boat. When the pair return to the dock they are offered a position on the camp's sailing team and they excitedly accept.

Gary está emocionado de ir al campamento de verano, este será el primer año en que tendrá la edad suficiente para tomar lecciones de navegación. Gary pasa su primer día con sus amigos, cada uno de ellos discutiendo la actividad que más esperan. El hermano de Gary quiere aprender tiro con arco mientras que su amigo Hiro quiere aprender fútbol. Al día siguiente, Gary y su compañero de navegación Maury comienzan sus lecciones, su instructor está impresionado con su progreso y los deja navegar solos mientras enseña a los demás. Mientras Gary y Maury navegan, ven a los amigos de Gary realizar las actividades que disfrutan y los animan desde el barco. Cuando la pareja regresa al muelle, se les ofrece un puesto en el equipo de navegación del campamento y aceptan con entusiasmo.

VOCABULARY

Orientation: Una introducción, como guía para adaptarse a un nuevo entorno, empleo, actividad o similar.

Outdoorsman: Una persona dedicada a los deportes al aire libre y actividades recreativas, como el senderismo, la caza, la pesca o la acampada.

Groggy: Aturdido y debilitado, como por falta de sueño.

Fiberglass: Material que consiste en fibras de vidrio finas enmarañadas.

Content: Satisfecho.

QUESTIONS

1. Who is Gary's brother?

A) Hiro.

B) Maury.

C) Jake.

D) Ben.

E) It doesn't say.

2. How old is Gary?

A) 15.

B) 12.

C) 14.

D) 13.

E) 16.

3. Who enjoys soccer?

A) Hiro.

B) Maury.

C) Jake.

D) Ben.

E) It doesn't say.

4. What is the name of the camp?

A) Camp Greenlake.

B) Camp Green lake.

C) Lake Green Camp.

D) Greenwood's.

E) Camp Greylocke.

5. Who is Gary's partner?

A) Hiro.

B) Maury.

C) Jake.

D) Ben.

E) It doesn't say.

Camping

Cassie could feel the cool evening air of autumn as she struggled with her bundle of sticks. It was getting late and Cassie and her friends had neglected to prepare a fire for their camp tonight, so they would all be cold. They had lost track of time that day, their long hike to the lake being filled with fun and **merriment** but little attention was paid to the time as they had journeyed. She could hear her friends crash through the debris on the forest floor as they too rushed to complete their tasks before dark as well. Arthurs footsteps were a heavy thud as he stomped through the woods, Cassie thought she could probably hear him from a mile away with how loud he was. His large frame and strength meant he was looking for the largest branches, the main source of fuel for their campfire tonight. Quieter were the steps of her sister Marge, who as the youngest and smallest member of their camping party was looking for smaller twigs and dry moss, the perfect starter to any good fire.

Cassie felt like the bundle in her arms was heavy enough, not to mention the last of the sun's light was disappearing over the tree line, she made her way back to the campsite. The fire would soon be burning as planned, in the center of a circle of small trees where they had set up camp. It would warm the ground and tents as it burned, creating a nice, cozy fire to sit and chat with friends. **Muffled** voices came from just beyond the tall pines opposite the camp as Cassie arrived depositing her fire wood, Marge and Arthur must be coming back together she thought to herself. Sure enough they entered the campsite, appearing from behind a bush, they seemed to be in the middle of conversation and Cassie sat by the fire pit next to her small branches waiting for them to finish. Marge was true to her talkative nature and in the middle of explaining her new middle school's local drama to a very patient Arthur who nodded at the appropriate intervals as Marge explained the ins and outs of her school like it was the politics of a royal family. Cassie noticed that Arthur barely seemed weighed down by the weight of the four large logs he was carrying, clearly her friend had been putting in his time at the gym since he had made it to his senior year's elite team for American Football. He dropped the logs with a loud thud next to Cassie's sticks and Marge deposited her kindling between his and Cassie's two wood piles.

The three got comfortable around the fire pit but there was precious little time to waste, the sun had disappeared over the horizon and what little light was left would soon be gone. Already Cassie found it hard to see beyond the campsite, the surrounding trees blending into the dark shadows behind them. All of the group knew how to start a fire, growing up in a small town in the woods tended to have that effect on people but Marge had recently finished her girl groups camping certificate and was eager to be the conductor of the event. "Cassie, place your sticks in the pit, make sure to give them height and a bit of space and don't forget to place the driest ones on the bottom." Commanded Marge, trying her best to speak with authority on the subject. Arthur and Cassie exchanged quick glances at each other, smiling as they did. Marge was still young and Arthur had known her for so long that he viewed her like a little sister as well, her new found confidence was cute. With the initial sticks properly arranged Marge began to place the smaller ones where she could, and filling the areas in between with small bundles of dry moss, before long they had a small **teepee** shaped pyramid ready to burn. Arthur did the honors of lighting the fire, using his lighter to start the kindling. The raspy sound of the flint of his lighter was preceded by the small flames at key areas of the wood pyramid. Before long a small smoky fire began to burn, the moss giving off plenty of smoke that blew between Cassie and Marge, causing them both to cough lightly and rub their eyes. Arthur laughed as he placed the first of the logs on the fire, before long it started to burn. With most of the moss gone the smoke cleared and allowed the group to enjoy their warm fire just as the last of the natural light disappeared and it truly became night.

Cassie warmed her hands by the fire, it wasn't unpleasantly cold but she could see a faint mist from her breath when she breathed out. Marge noticed and the sister engaged in a silly game with her, each would take turns to see who could breathe the biggest mist cloud like when they were both young. Each of the girls pretended to be dragons as they did roaring into the night after each breath. Laughter surrounded the campfire, Arthur had even bought his special kettle and before long all three of them were enjoying steaming hot mugs of cocoa around the fire. The crackle and burn from the fire provided a perfect background noise and was accompanied by the sounds of small animals in the forest. **Periodically** the conversation would stop and they would stare into the fire, watching the wood burn away its energy in flame. Each one of them took turns to **stoke** and tend to the fire, adding Cassie's branches or one of Arthur's logs as needed.

Before long the moon was high in the sky, its crescent shape illuminating the clearing almost as much as the fire, Marge was the first to yawn, it was getting late and the group agreed it was time for bed. Cassie and Marge got into their tents while Arthur waited for the fire to die down enough for him to snuff out the embers with some loose dirt before retiring to his own tent. That night the three of them happily dreamed, content and full of cocoa. They dreamt of the adventures they would have on this trip. It was another day's hike to the lake they were headed to and even though everything had turned out okay tonight all three of them made a mental note that next time they would keep an eye on the time and set up their fire a little earlier.

SUMMARY

Cassie, Marge and Arthur go on a camp trip to a lake a few days away from their small town, they have a great day hiking but lose track of time and have to rush to create a fire. Cassie has some time to herself as she gathers wood before returning to the campsite. When Marge and Arthur return, the group talk for a bit before starting to assemble the fire pit with Marge taking charge. Once the fire is underway the group enjoy each other's company and some hot cocoa before going to bed, as

Cassie gets ready to sleep she makes a note to manage the group's time better going forward.

Cassie, Marge y Arthur van de campamento a un lago a unos días de distancia de su pequeño pueblo. Tienen un gran día de caminata, pero pierden la noción del tiempo y tienen que apresurarse para encender el fuego. Cassie tiene algo de tiempo para sí misma mientras recoge leña antes de regresar al campamento. Cuando Marge y Arthur regresan, el grupo habla un poco antes de comenzar a armar el fuego con Marge a cargo. Una vez que el fuego está en marcha, el grupo disfruta de la compañía de los demás y de un poco de chocolate caliente antes de irse a la cama, mientras Cassie se prepara para dormir, toma nota para administrar mejor el tiempo del grupo en el futuro.

VOCABULARY

Merriment: Alegre o gozoso.

Muffled: Sonido suprimido.

Teepee: Tienda de campaña de los indios americanos, generalmente hecha de un marco cónico.

Periodically: Intervalos de tiempo regulares o algo regulares.

Stoke: Alimentar o avivar el fuego.

QUESTIONS

1. Where are the group traveling too?

A) The River.

B) The Beach.

C) The Lake.

D) The Forest.

E) The Mountain.

2. Who is grabbing the largest sticks for the fire?

A) Arthur.

B) Marge.

C) Cassie.

D) Andrew.

E) All of them.

3. What did Marge just complete before the trip?

A) Camping Certificate.

B) High school.

C) Preschool.

D) Camping Badge.

E) College.

4. What does Arthur make over the fire?

A) Tea.

B) Coffee.

C) Pancakes.

D) Chocolate.

E) Cocoa.

5. How many days do the group think it will take to reach the lake from the start?

A) 1.

B) 2.

C) 3.

D) 4.

E) They weren't sure.

Doctor Visit

Ned had never liked visiting the doctors. In fact it wouldn't be too **outrageous** to say that he hated going to the doctors, but his asthma was always a concern and required tests every six months or so. This did not stop him dreading it the entire time though, if anything it made it worse. He felt his stomach tie itself into knots whenever he and his mother would take the train to the hospital, his grip on the bar to keep himself steady on the train was **clammy** and a cold sweat would be on his brow. When the train would rattle into the familiar station he would almost have to force himself to move to the exit before the doors closed again. His legs felt like lead as they walked the short trip from the station to the hospital a few blocks away, his grip on his mothers hand tight searching for comfort as he faced the inevitable.

The hospital itself was a nice clean and modern building, it had been renovated a view years ago transformed into a shining mix of glass and steel gleaming in the sunlight. Ned felt as though it was a trick, outside were still the same ambulances, patients in wheelchairs and other things that made him nervous. After entering the main lobby to check in for their appointment Ned and his mother would walk down a small side street. The Hospital complex was so large it almost felt like its own neighborhood, the clinic that Ned frequented even had its own playground though Ned himself was often too nervous to be in the mood to play on it. The Clinic itself was a simple building, looking more like an old historical house than a medical facility. Ned had to admit that the comforting feeling of a home did put him slightly more at ease. The inside of the clinic was a simple office, two receptionists spent their time behind the main desk at the computer and the waiting room was furnished with comfy couches. Each of the receptionists, whose names were Jack and Diane, said hello to Ned by name. He had been coming here for four years now and had built up a kind relationship with them, they felt almost like an uncle and aunt. Jack would always sneakily slip Ned a lollipop, a gift usually reserved for the end of a visit but this way Ned got two! He always felt his mom was politely ignoring the small bribe given to him, she was probably happy that it helped put him at ease.

The wait was sometimes the hardest part of the trip to the doctor, sometimes the waiting room would be full of other children and their parents waiting for their turn and the wait felt like hours to Ned. Most children would go outside to play on the slide and monkey bars provided in the small playground. While Ned would as well occasionally after his visits were complete he was always too nervous to enjoy it himself beforehand. Instead Ned would busy himself with the toys provided in the waiting room, usually not getting much out of them since they were designed for a much younger age group then himself and either way were usually in less then good condition after years of constant play with other children. Sometimes he would read from the magazines provided, though they were usually a few months out of date and about things that did not interest him like celebrities or fashion, though some would occasionally have puzzles or crosswords that he would attempt.

Today though was a quick wait, it was the middle of the week and there was no one else in the waiting room, Ned had barely sat down before Doctor Clarence had appeared in the door to his office, ushering him in. Doctor Clarence was a red headed man of middle age, his hair short but a big bushy mustache covered his entire top lip. He had a calm and soothing bedside manner and it did wonders for Ned's state of mind.

The tests began as usual, a standard health check up before Ned's dreaded throat swab, his least favorite part of his visits. Doctor Clarence checked his heart beat with a stethoscope, placing it to Ned's chest before moving it occasionally, asking him to breathe in and out calmly. After that came the blood pressure test, a plastic ring like a deflated tube was placed around his arm before filling up with air, a sharp beep ringing out when it was done. Ned Wasn't sure how any of these tests worked, as far as he was concerned this was just a prelude to the main event. Sure enough Doctor Clarence turned around to grab his pen flashlight and swab, Ned reluctantly opened his mouth to prepare for the **invasive** procedure. As Doctor Clarence shined the light into Ned's open mouth Ned heard a surprised sound from his Doctor. Ned was concerned, what did this mean? Has his throat gotten worse? He was about to voice his concerns when Doctor Clarence let out a little chuckle.

"Good news my young friend, your throat is fine, it seems the **medication** has worked!" Said the doctor. Ned was shocked, he almost wanted to hug his doctor. They finished his exam and Ned flew out to the waiting room to hug his mother, he told her the good news and her eyes lit up in joy. Ned went to say goodbye to the Doctor, Jack and Diane but almost stopped himself when he realized that this was going to be the last time he would see them! Ned suddenly felt an unexpected wave of sadness wash over him, he wasn't ready to say goodbye; he had known them all for four years and become quite attached. He did say goodbye and made sure to thank them as much as he could for all their kindness and hard work, as he and his mother left the clinic he thought to himself: 'How strange that I'm going to miss the pace I dreaded going'. Ned and his mother walked to the train station, happy that he was healthy but he would miss his friends at the clinic.

SUMMARY

Ned and his mother go to the doctors to get a check up on his asthma which requires constant check ins. Ned dislikes going to the doctors due to the nature of the invasive procedures and as they travel recounts all the reasons he doesn't like going. When Ned and his mother arrive they wait in the waiting room where he recounts how he usually passes the time before his appointment after being greeted by the friendly receptionists. Once it's time for his appointment Ned's doctor is surprised to find his condition has resolved itself and Ned no longer needs any procedures. Ned's happiness about this news is only tempered by him realizing he had come to enjoy his doctor and the receptionists and will miss seeing them regularly.

Ned y su madre acuden a los médicos para que les controlen el asma, lo que requiere controles constantes. A Ned no le gusta ir al médico debido a la naturaleza de los procedimientos invasivos y, mientras viajan, cuenta todas las razones por las que no le gusta ir. Cuando Ned y su madre llegan, esperan en la sala de espera donde él cuenta cómo suele pasar el tiempo antes de su cita después de ser recibido por los amables recepcionistas. Una vez que llega el momento de su cita, el médico de Ned se sorprende al descubrir que su condición se ha resuelto por sí sola y que Ned ya no necesita ningún procedimiento. La felicidad de Ned por esta noticia solo se ve atenuada cuando se da cuenta de que había venido a disfrutar de su médico y de las recepcionistas y que extrañará verlos con regularidad.

VOCABULARY

Outrageous: Muy audaz, inusual y sorprendente.

Clammy: Desagradablemente húmedo y pegajoso o viscoso al tacto.

Invasive: Que implique la introducción de instrumentos u otros objetos en el cuerpo o en las cavidades corporales.

Medication: Una sustancia utilizada para el tratamiento médico, especialmente un medicamento o droga.

Frequented: Visitado a menudo o habitualmente.

QUESTIONS

1. What condition does Ned have?

A) Asthma.

B) Poor Eyesight.

C) Headaches.

D) Sore throat.

E) A cold.

2. What is the male receptionist's name?

A) Ned.

B) Jack.

C) Clarence.

D) Jim.

E) James.

3. What color Is Doctor Clarence's hair?

A) Blonde.

B) Black.

C) Brown.

D) Red.

E) Gray.

4. Who has a mustache?

A) Ned.

B) Jack.

C) Clarence.

D) Jim.

E) James.

5. Why does Ned not enjoy the toys in the waiting room?

A) They are broken.

B) He is too old.

C) They are too complex.

D) He's too nervous.

E) There are none.

Grandma's Parakeet

Jordan knew his mum was sad. It had been 3 months since his grandma had passed and the house had been quieter since, the only new sound being Grandma's **parakeet** named Jack that Jordan's family had inherited. He was also worried about his dad's new job. He had heard his parents talking about it at night, that he was going back to the city. Jordan was pretty sure that his Dad was not happy about it, as the new city was further away than the old one and his job would **entail** much more. Jordan had also heard that the job was in the military, where he would probably be working on a ship, or in some sort of research lab. So he knew he would be away for a long time. His mum had told him that she was worried she might get lonely with both Jordan's Father and grandmother gone. Jordan tried hard to improve his mother's mood but everything he did seemed to only create a little joy before his mum would become sad again.

Eventually Jordan's dad did go to the city for work, but he would try to visit every other week and the money he sent home helped keep the household going, along with Jordan's mother taking some part time work at the local grocery store. With everyone home less often it fell on Jordan to help maintain the house more. Every day when he came home from school he would turn on the old radio his grandma had kept in the living room feed Jack as he swung on his perch and listen to music as he cleaned the apartment, he would sweep the floors and do any dishes from breakfast and the night before. Once he was done cleaning he would take any instructions his mother had left on how to finish the meal she had prepared for dinner the night before and begin his homework, it was often at this time his mother would arrive home from work and take over preparing dinner, letting Jordan focus on his studies.

This changed however one cold autumn day, Jordan had arrived home from school and begun his cleaning when a classic song came on the radio, a pop hit from the early eighties his grandmother had loved. He noticed Jack perk up in his cage, his bright white feathers extending like a **mohawk** as he turned his head to the radio and started to bob up and down in excitement. To Jordan's surprise Jack began to sing, squawks turning to half formed words **mimicking** the lyrics of the song on the radio. Jordan knew Parakeets could mimic human language but Jack was a surprisingly quiet bird since Jordan's grandma had passed and had never talked in whole sentences like this before.

Jordan had a fantastic idea, he finally knew what he had to do to cheer up his mother! He finished his cleaning and ran down to the local music store, an old shop two blocks away. The stores inside felt old, the owner was a nice man who had known his grandma ever since he opened the shop many years ago, both of them bonding over their shared love of 'the classics' as they called them. Jordan explained his plan to the owner of the store and his face lit up at the idea. The whole neighborhood loved Jordan's family and were sad to hear of their recent troubles. Jordan and the owner walked down the aisles of music, it felt almost like a time machine, CD's turning into cassette tapes and records as they went further back into the store. It was at the cassettes almost at the back of the store that they stopped and the owner plucked out a cassette tape with a faded cover. "This is from the seventies, some of your sweet grandma's favorite music" the owner of the store said. Jordan was amazed his mother hadn't even been born yet when this was released. He couldn't imagine his sweet grandma that young, even younger than what his mother was now! Jordan reached into his pockets or his allowance but the owner shook his head as he gave Jordan the tape. He was more than happy to help, he said smiling, adding that 'no one was going to buy this old tape anyway' with a soft chuckle.

Jordan raced home, he still had a few moments to start dinner before his mother got home from work. He began the stew that his mother had prepared last night and just had time to put the tape in his grandma's old radio as he heard his mother's key click in the lock of the front door.

As his mother entered he could see the confusion in her face, but it swiftly turned to a smile as she saw Jack sing along to the songs on the radio, the bird clearly well practiced in the songs her own mother loved. She came to Jordan embracing him in a big hug.

"Did you do this my son?" she asked.

"Yes mum, I've been wanting to make you happy since grandma and was hoping this would do it." Jordan replied. He looked up at his mother and was confused, he could see tears forming in her eyes but a smile on her face.

"What's wrong?" He asked.

"Nothing my darling boy, sometimes tears can mean you're happy, it's been too long since I've let myself remember your grandma without being sad." his mother said before continuing "now dance with me for a little bit while we remember your sweet grandma."

Jordan and his mother danced for the whole tape as Jack the parrot sang in the background, both of them finally completely happy for the first time in months. It was good to remember that as long as you held someone's memory with love in your heart they were never truly gone.

SUMMARY

After Jordan's Grandmother passed away he began to worry about his mother becoming lonely since his father also had to move to the city for work. One day as he cleans the house he notices that the Parakeet the family had inherited from their grandmother begins to sing along to a classic song on the radio and this gives him an idea to cheer his mother up. Jordan makes his way to the local record store and gets a tape of classic songs. When his mother arrives home he plays the music and the fond memories of her mother make her cry with joy. Happy to have such a fond memory of her mother back Jordan's mother ask him to dance with her while the music plays.

Después de que la abuela de Jordan falleciera, comenzó a preocuparse de que su madre se sintiera sola ya que su padre también tuvo que mudarse a la ciudad por trabajo. Un día mientras limpia la casa se da cuenta de que el Periquito que la familia había heredado de su abuela comienza a cantar una canción clásica en la radio y esto le da una idea para animar a su madre. Jordan se dirige a la tienda de discos local y consigue una cinta de canciones clásicas. Cuando su madre llega a casa, él pone la música y los buenos recuerdos de su madre la hacen llorar de alegría. Feliz de tener un recuerdo tan grato de su madre. La madre de Jordan le pide que baile con ella mientras suena la música.

VOCABULARY

Parakeet: Un periquito es cualquiera de las muchas especies de loros de tamaño pequeño a mediano.

Entail: Involucrar algo como una parte o consecuencia necesaria o inevitable.

Maintain: Causar o permitir que una condición o estado de cosas continúe.

Mimicking: Imitar a alguien o sus acciones o palabras.

Mohawk: Un peinado con una franja central angosta de cabello generalmente erguido y los lados de la cabeza rapados.

QUESTIONS

1. What kind of bird does the family inherit?

A) Cockatoo.

B) Duck.

C) Starling.

D) Budgie.

E) Parakeet.

2. Who has passed away?

A) Mother.

B) Aunt.

C) Grandmother.

D) Grandfather.

E) Father.

3. Where does Jack's father go?

A) The city.

B) The countryside.

C) Overseas.

D) Next door.

E) It doesn't say.

4. What decade of songs are on the tape Jack buys?

A) 60's.

B) 70's.

C) 80's.

D) 90's.

E) Various.

5. How much does the tape cost?

A) $5.

B) $4.

C) $3.

D) $7.

E) Its free.

Island Experience

Richard felt the cool sea spray on his face as he stood on the bow of the ferry. The air cooled him and he shivered, considering heading back into the passenger cabin but he was too excited he needed to be the first in his family to see the Island. Richard's family was going to an island in the South Pacific, a small island off the coast of Australia. He was going there with his mother and his sister. Richard had never been to the island before and he didn't know what it looked like. All he could see was the blue of the sky and water meeting at the horizon and the white of a sea of clouds above. He had no idea what the island looked like. Earlier his mother had told him that it had the shape of a big pyramid and that the people who lived there did so in the shade of the massive volcano. Though the volcano was long since dormant, not erupting in hundreds of years. There had been a man on a boat that had gone to the island regularly and offered to show them to their hotel when they arrived, an offer Richard's mother readily accepted.

It wasn't long before Richard saw it, a small green pin prick at first, directly ahead of them. Soon it had become larger, the size of a jewel, like a green emerald Richard thought. It wasn't long before the island was close enough for Richard to see the ferry dock and the small **colonial** town surrounding it, with the jungle beyond leading up to a steep mountainside and all the way to the top of the volcano's rim beyond.

He looked around at the new view before going down to the passenger section of the ferry to meet with his family before they disembarked.

"I don't understand why we're going here." His sister said as the boat pulled up to dock. Richard's sister was 10 years older than him and not a huge fan of remote locations, instead preferring resorts and large cities to unwind in.

"It is the best place for a vacation, me and your father used to come here whenever we could." His mother replied.

Disembarking took some time with their luggage, the kind stranger from the boat helping them load their bags into the back of his car before driving them to their hotel just outside of the central part of town. The kind man refused even a tip saying that it was just **custom** on the island to help others, hoping they'd do the same if someone needed it during their stay. Before he left he gave Richard's mother their number in case the family needed anything else. The family settled in quickly to the small hotel, Richard enjoyed cooling off in the small pool in the courtyard as his sister suntanned and his mother read a book in the shade.

The next day was spent in the small town that Richard learned was called 'Emerald Cove', Richard's family spending the day in the historical part of town, walking the streets and exploring their vacation destination. By the end, there was only a single street in sight, leading out of town and wrapping around the side of the mountain.

"That will be our adventure tomorrow." said Richard's mother as the family turned back and made their way to the hotel. That night Richard struggled to sleep, he was excited by the prospect of exploring what was beyond the bend in the road. 'What was beyond?' He wondered, imagining ancient ruins or dense jungle, fantasizing about being an intrepid explorer he finally felt sleep gently take him.

The following day Richard was up early, his family were just getting out of bed but he was already up and ready to go, when his family were ready Richard quickly made his way downstairs to their rented Jeep they had gotten from town the day before. He opened the front door and was surprised to see the man from the boat who helped them to their hotel!

"Oh honey glad to see you've met Terry again." his mum said as they reached the Jeep, "He kindly volunteered to show us around the island today" she continued. Richard was ecstatic, he couldn't wait to have a real local show them around the island.

The trip started off slow, it turned out just around the street bend from yesterday was farmland. The farm's primary purpose was primarily to grow food for locals to eat but some tropical fruits were harvested and sent back to the mainland as Terry explained. Richard let himself get distracted by the farm animals as they drove. It was mostly sheep he saw as they passed field after field but occasionally he'd see horses or cows in one of the pastures, he'd watch as their large heads followed the car on its journey around the Island. It wasn't too long though before the Island farms gave way to jungle, first a few trees but soon the Jeep was surrounded on all sides by **exotic** tropical plants and trees. It was much different from the pine forests back home.

Terry had saved the best for last though as they drove, he took a trail road through the jungle, the rougher terrain jostling the passengers inside. But it didn't take long before the path began to scale the mountain and Terry drove very slowly and carefully up the side of the volcano. Every now and then the dense trees parted as they drove and Richard could see breathtaking views of the forest below. His family could as well, he could hear the clicks of their cameras behind him as he stared out the window at the wonderful view. Once they reached the top the family could not believe the view in front of them, for 360 degrees around they had a perfect view of the ocean and the island below. The green jungle sloped down the mountainside into the perfect crystal blue of the ocean below. This was almost as good as any ancient ruin or secret treasure Richard thought. As Terry took a photo of the family, Richard was full of joy knowing that he and his family would create many happy memories on this island. He knew almost without a doubt that he would be **begging** his mother to come back to the emerald cove again next year, who knew maybe he'd find treasures next time!

SUMMARY

Richard goes with his family to a nearby island for a holiday. They take the ferry and his sister mentions the island is very remote, upon arriving a kindly local helps them with their luggage before taking them to the hotel for the night. The next day the family toured the city before resolving to explore further later. The kindly local takes them on a drive culminating at the top of the mountain where the family marvel at the view.

Richard se va de vacaciones con su familia a una isla cercana. Toman el ferry y su hermana menciona que la isla es muy remota, al llegar, un local amable los ayuda con su equipaje antes de llevarlos al hotel para pasar la noche. Al día siguiente, la familia recorrió la ciudad antes de decidir explorar más tarde. El amable lugareño los lleva a un viaje que culmina en la cima de la montaña donde la familia se maravilla con la vista.

VOCABULARY

Colonial: Relativo o característico de una colonia o época colonial.

Begging: Pedir algo a alguien con seriedad o humildad.

Exotic: Originario o característico de un país extranjero distante.

Disembarking: Leave a ship, aircraft, or other vehicle.

Custom: A traditional and widely accepted way of behaving or doing something that is specific to a particular society, place, or time.

QUESTIONS

1. Where is the Island near?

A) Asia.

B) Australia.

C) Austria.

D) Hawaii.

E) England.

2. What is the town on the island's name?

A) Hidden Port.

B) Secret Jewel.

C) Green Cove.

D) Emerald Cove.

E) Emerald Beach.

3. What is the name of the friendly local?

A) Richard.

B) Eric.

C) Terry.

D) Terrance.

E) Taylor.

4. What kind of forests were common in Terry's home?

A) Pine.

B) Oak.

C) Willow.

D) Evergreen.

E) Spruce.

5. What kind of Jewel does the island remind Terry of?

A) Diamond.

B) Jade.

C) Ruby.

D) Amber.

E) Emerald.

Kim's Beach

Kim's favorite place to go on holiday was the beach near her Grandparents' house on the coast. The beach was just a few miles from where they lived in southern California and many members of her family lived nearby. Kim was always happy to see her Grandparents and cousins, they were often her favorite part of the trip because they were always there to greet her. She would often spend the night at either her cousins playing card games or at her grandparents house reading books. One day during one of her holidays Kim and her cousins' were walking on the path along the beach to their Grandparents' house when a giant crab came out of the sand and pinched her feet with its claws! Kim was so shocked she ran the rest of the way to her Grandparents house.

"I was so **startled**! It got my big toe!" Kim said to her Grandmother as she hopped into their beachside house.

"What was that? Did you get hurt?" her Grandmother asked.

"No, I just got a little bit scared," Kim answered laughing, her shock fading and turning into good humor. That day was the start of how Kim got to know her Grandmother a little better. Her name was Judith, when she was young she was an engineer, a scientist, an inventor. She was also the first person in her entire family to ever go to university. Kim's Grandmother was very kind and very proud of her granddaughter. Her parents were very loving and supportive of her as well, as she was their only child, to the point that her mother would cry whenever they left her at her Grandmothers for summer break.

When Kim told her about the crab her Grandmother's eyes had lit up with a twinkle. Kim's Grandmother went to her desk, a very old antique made by her own Grandmother many years ago and pulled out some books. Placing them on the coffee table and sitting with her granddaughter she motioned to Kim to look closer.

"These are my old textbooks from when I was a scientist, do you know what kind of scientist I was Kim?" asked her Grandmother.

"No grandma, were you a crab scientist?' Kim asked curiously.

Her grandma chuckled "not quite dear. I was a **marine biologist**, I studied all sorts of aquatic life, crabs, dolphins, sharks. Anything that lived near or in the water I would study." Kim was interested in her grandma's answer, and soon was amazed at the things her Grandmother knew about the ocean. Opening the book to a marked page Kim's Grandmother began to tell her all about the crabs that lived on the beach nearby. Kim was fascinated by their life cycle, how they lived long lives, how they could breathe underwater and in the air and how their strong claws (that she now had very personal experience with.) could regrow if given enough time. Kim was also very interested in her Grandmother's work. In fact, she was fascinated with all things marine.

Four years later Kim at the age of seventeen was already preparing to go to university. Kim had been inspired that day all those years ago with the dream of one day working for a company that specialized in marine biology and marine exploration. That Summer she drove herself to her Grandma's house to enjoy summer vacation with her and her fun loving cousins one last time before heading away to university. She wondered if the crab was still living near the path from the beach to her grandmas and if it ever thought of Kim as the giant creature that gave it a big fright, knowing now how timid and non aggressive crabs were. Kim walked to the house with one of their cousins to see how their grandma was, she was getting older now and rarely left the house. Instead preferring to relax on her porch in a big comfy chair reading books and listening to the waves crash against the nearby shore. As they approached the house from over the sand dune Kim could see her at her usual spot in her chair. Kim and her cousin waved to their grandma, their grandma waved back, her eyesight still as sharp as ever.

They had tea and both Kim and her cousin told their grandma tales of what they were up to, their plans for the summer and their futures. Kim's cousin Stacy wanted to focus on her tan on the beach for a few weeks before enjoying a year **abroad** in Europe and coming home to train to be a nurse.

"What are your plans Kim?" Her Grandmother asked, Kim told her all about her plans to go to university and become a marine biologist just like her Grandmother did. Kim's grandma beamed proudly, she was so happy to see her little granddaughter grow up and follow in her footsteps.

"I'm so happy to hear that Kim, in fact after that day you met the crab I could sense that you may follow your passion just like me." She smiled, pausing to build excitement before continuing. "That's why I've gone to the town council and paid a small fee to rename the stretch of beach in front of the house 'Kim's Beach' so you'll always have a part of the ocean as your home to come back to."

Kim was **overcome** with emotion, she couldn't think of a better gift, she hugged her grandma, kissing her on the cheek as she did.

"Thank you so much grandma, it really means the world to me that you did that." Kim said, wiping away tears from her eyes as she was so happy.

"Don't just thank me." Her grandma said. "There's a crab out there on that beach and if it wasn't for him you never would have found your passion, you're going to need help if you want to find and thank him as well." Everyone in the room laughed, Kim considered it. Her grandma was probably right, if it wasn't for that sneaky crab all those years ago she may have never discovered her love of the ocean with her grandma, or gotten a beach named after her.

"Me and Stacy will go for a swim" said Kim, "watch us from the porch grandma, we'll let you know if we see him." Kim and her cousin grabbed their towels and headed for the surf, setting foot on the beach once again. Kim's Beach.

SUMMARY

Kim is excited to visit her Grandma while on holiday with her cousins nearby, after a shocking encounter with a crab on the beaches she rushes to her Grandma's house. Once there she explains what happened and her Grandma responds by sharing her knowledge of crabs and other marine life with her Granddaughter, turning her fear into curiosity. Years later Kim returns to her grandma excited to start her training to become a marine biologist, Kim's Grandmother reveals that in honor of her granddaughter's success she has named part of the beach after her. Kim is honored by this and proceeds to go enjoy said beach with her cousin.

Kim está emocionada de visitar a su abuela mientras está de vacaciones con sus primos, después de un impactante encuentro con un cangrejo en las playas, se apresura para ir a la casa de su abuela. Una vez allí, explica lo sucedido y su abuela responde compartiendo su conocimiento sobre los cangrejos y otras especies marinas con su nieta, convirtiendo su miedo en curiosidad. Años más tarde, Kim regresa con su abuela emocionada de comenzar su formación para convertirse en bióloga marina. La abuela de Kim revela que, en honor al éxito de su nieta, le ha puesto su nombre a parte de la playa. Kim se siente honrada por esto y procede a disfrutar de dicha playa con su prima.

VOCABULARY

Startled: Sentir o mostrar shock o alarma repentina.

Overcome: Tener éxito en un desafío difícil o llenarse de emociones fuertes.

Marine: Del mar.

Biologist: Un experto o estudiante de la rama de la ciencia relacionada con los organismos vivos.

Abroad: En el extranjero.

QUESTIONS

1. Where does Kim's grandmother live?

A) Northern California.

B) Southern California.

C) Northern Colorado.

D) Southern Colorado.

E) South Carolina.

2. What scares Kim on the way to her Grandmother's?

A) A Shark.

B) A Fish.

C) A Crab.

D) A Seagull.

E) A Jellyfish.

3. When does Kim return to her Grandmother's house?

A) 1 Year later.

B) 2 Years later.

C) 3 Years later.

D) 4 Years later.

E) 5 Years later.

4. What does Kim's cousin want to be?

A) A Marine Biologist.

B) A Pilot.

C) A Stewardess.

D) A Doctor.

E) A Nurse.

5. What is Kim's grandmother's name?

A) Judith.

B) Judy.

C) Juliet.

D) Jamie.

E) Julia.

Lost in New York

Jessie had finally made it and was ready for an amazing day. From her small home of Modoc in California she had traveled by bus all the way to New York City! It was a grueling multi day long trip in a hot bus but it was worth it to see her best friend Daphne, who had invited her as a plus one to Daphne's aunts wedding. It had been years since her friend had moved to New York City after her father had gotten an important job there and moved. Jessie forgot what Daphne's father did, she thought it had something to do with banking or computers. Jessie had cashed in all her favors with her own parents to have them fund her trip to New York as an early eighteenth birthday present but it had all felt worth it the moment her bus had pulled into the underground stations of the Port Authority Terminal, New York's central transport **hub** for buses.

Jessie had organized a schedule, she had a whole day to explore the city while Daphne helped her aunt prepare for the wedding. Jessie felt invigorated, feeling the cool October morning air on her face as she left the terminal and hailed a cab to her hotel so she could leave her bags and freshen up before getting ready to see what the city had to offer. She was very happy to wash the last two days of nonstop bus rides off, there was only so much body odor deodorant could cover! Her hotel was perfectly **situated**, she had chosen it specifically for its accessibility to the sights she wanted to see, along with it being small and inexpensive it was situated on East 50th street, only two blocks from the river and with a view of Brooklyn from the top floor.

Jessie had decided to spend the day crisscrossing the city seeing the sites and working her way down to the harbor and the Statue of Liberty. She began in Central Park and concluded that it looked just like the movies she watched back home. Well-kept paths intersected green and pleasant fields flanked with giant oak trees, Jessie watched with delight as small chipmunks and squirrels ran up and down the trees, taking food offered by tourists such as herself. Cautiously taking nuts from their hands before racing up the trees occasionally chased by other park wildlife. Remembering her time limit Jessie reluctantly left the park, making her way to Times Square the bustling heart of the city.

This was a very different experience from her peaceful park visit! The square was filled to the brim with people, Jessie felt pushed around like she was in a stream and struggled to find her bearings, almost like being pushed by a strong current she found it difficult to stand her ground. The lights and billboards on the towers reached up into the sky, Jessie had to strain her neck to see all the way to the top. She had never been around such tall buildings, Modoc's tallest building barely reached ten stories tall and was nowhere near as big as these huge buildings, some of them taking up entire city blocks!

Feeling overwhelmed by the noise and commotion Jessie had to find a moment to collect herself otherwise she thought she might panic! Thankfully the opportunity came at her next destination, the Rockefeller **plaza** was practically deserted compared to the nearby Times Square and Jessie took the time to eat a slice of pizza from a nearby vendor as she enjoyed the relative peace of the plaza. She had heard that the pizza in New York City couldn't be beaten, she hadn't been to many places known for their pizza but she could definitely tell it was better than her local restaurant back home, although it was a lot greasier. Feeling more collected and with a full stomach she made her way to one of the attractions that she had been wanting to see the most, the Empire State building.

It was an imposing structure, this close she couldn't quite see the top but this only made her more excited to reach it, she entered the lobby and bought her ticket to the top. At the top of the Empire State Building the view took Jessie's breathe away, she could see the entire city from here, less than a handful of buildings in the city were taller and she had an almost unblocked view. She could see the state of New Jersey in the distance and thought to herself how there was no building back home so tall that she could see another state.

There was only time for one more visit before the wedding **rehearsal** but Jessie knew exactly what she wanted to see, hailing one more cab she rushed to the bottom of the city to see the Statue of liberty, even though it seemed so small from so far away Jessie marveled at its beauty. Placing a quarter in the slot of a nearby **telescope** she pointed its viewfinder to the statue and appreciated the beauty of its construction. Its pale green color blended beautifully with the dark blue of the ocean behind it. She watched as ferries full of tourists floated past, she wondered if they knew that the statue hadn't always been green but instead the light brown of copper! She remembered learning that fact in school and wondered what it must have looked like when it was first built.

Jessie was suddenly faced by a crisis, she checked her purse and no longer had enough money for a cab to the wedding rehearsal! Thinking quickly she ran to the nearest subway, she had never been underground before and was more than excited to experience one of the world's oldest underground rail systems. Paying her fare and reading the map to figure out where to go, she quickly boarded a leaving train. She tapped her feet impatiently as the train sped towards her destination, it would be a close call she thought as it pulled into the station she needed. Jumping off the train Jessie ran back to her hotel with barely enough time to spare, dressing in her formal wear before heading to the reception nearby. Almost out of breath from excitement she entered the wedding hall. What an exciting day she had, Jessie couldn't wait to see her friend Daphne and tell her all about it, they had so much to catch up on and she couldn't wait to tell her about her adventure around the city.

SUMMARY

Jessie travels across the United States of America to see her best friend Daphne in New York for Daphne's Aunts wedding. The two girls had not seen each other since Daphne moved from Modoc California. Jessie spends the day sightseeing while Daphne helps her Aunt prepare for the wedding, traveling to see many of New York's famous sights. Eventually

Jessie loses track of time before having to rush back, forced to take the subway due to not having enough money for a Taxi. Jessie looks forward to telling her friend about the adventure as they catch up.

Jessie viaja por los Estados Unidos de América para ver a su mejor amiga Daphne en Nueva York para la boda de las tías de Daphne. Las dos chicas no se habían visto desde que Daphne se mudó de Modoc, California. Jessie pasa el día haciendo turismo mientras Daphne ayuda a su tía a prepararse para la boda y viaja para ver muchos de los lugares más famosos de Nueva York. Eventualmente, Jessie pierde la noción del tiempo antes de tener que regresar corriendo, obligada a tomar el metro debido a que no tiene suficiente dinero para un taxi. Jessie espera contarle a su amiga sobre la aventura mientras se ponen al día.

VOCABULARY

Hub: El centro o eje de una actividad o región.

Situated: Situarse en un determinado lugar o posición.

Rehearsal: El acto de practicar en preparación para una actuación pública.

Telescope: Un instrumento óptico diseñado para hacer que los objetos distantes parezcan más cercanos.

Plaza: Una plaza pública, mercado o espacio abierto similar.

QUESTIONS

1. Where does Daphne come from?

A) New York.

B) Modoc.

C) Boston.

D) Philadelphia.

E) Madison.

2. What is the second landmark Jessie sees?

A) Times Square.

B) Empire State Building.

C) Rockefeller Plaza.

D) The Statue of Liberty.

E) Central Park.

3. How does Jessie get back to the hotel?

A) Taxi.

B) Walking.

C) Bicycle.

D) Ferry.

E) Subway.

4. Who is getting married?

A) Daphne's Mother.

B) Daphne's Uncle.

C) Daphne's Aunt.

D) Daphne's Father.

E) Daphne's Sister.

5. Why does Jessie have trouble getting back to her hotel?

A) Not enough money.

B) It's late.

C) She forgot where it was.

D) It's closed.

E) It's raining.

Movie Night

'Tonight was the night' thought Reggie as he got dressed in his room. He'd begged and pleaded with his parents for almost two whole months, he'd kept his grades up, done his chores and made sure they knew it until finally only two days ago they **relented**.

"You can go to the movie night with your friends, and you can even take the car but if there's a scratch on it or you're home after midnight then you can say goodbye to going out for the rest of the year." The words hung in Reggie's mind as he got ready, his best clothes he'd spent all week picking out arrayed before him. It would be a tight squeeze to fit everything in before twelve he thought but he had planned extensively, even checking a map! Picking up his friends Jay and Lisa, going to the drive-in, dropping them back and finally getting home would be difficult to do in time but he'd be home by quarter to midnight with fifteen whole minutes to spare if his plan was correct. He'd been so excited and **determined** to **organize** his first true taste of freedom that his driver's license he had recently gotten had to offer that he'd forgotten what the movie was even about! It was Halloween so naturally the drive-in would be playing a horror movie, but as he wracked his brain trying to remember while he descended the stairs to say good-bye to his parents he was coming up short. 'Was it zombies or aliens? Maybe it was both!' He wondered to himself, already filled with excitement and eagerness to see his friends.

"See you soon Mom, I'll be back before you know it, I swear." Reggie said as he kissed his mother on the cheek making sure to be the best possible son today, he wasn't leaving anything to chance. A shadow loomed behind him, his dad was waiting at the door.

"Remember what I said Reginald, no scratches and be home by twelve." he said, dangling the keys before his eager son. "We're putting a lot of trust in you tonight young man." he continued.

"Of course, dad you know you can trust me" Reggie replied as he took the keys and said his goodbyes. Reggie was already struggling not to dash to the car in his excitement, instead making his best effort to calmly leave out the front door to the driveway.

Reggie stared at the vehicle in the driveway, there she was the family car. A modest vehicle but well maintained by his father and tonight it was Reggie's path to independence. At fifteen years old it was almost as old as Reggie himself but tonight it felt like a luxury chariot as Reggie got into its driver's seat.

"Check the handbrake and adjust your mirrors, keep your hands at ten and two." Reggie said, repeating the mantra he had heard dozens of times from his father as he had trained him for his license test. With the key in the ignition Reggie felt the car's engine vibrate into life. He gently reversed out into his neighborhood, it was barely past 6 so trick or treaters had barely started to begin their festivities. It was a quiet and gentle drive all the way to the pick-up point he had organized with Jay and Lisa ahead of time, or at least it would have been if Reggie wasn't playing his favorite songs at full volume on the way.

"Geez Reg we must have heard you for a mile before we saw you, turn that stuff down" laughed Jay as he slid into the passenger seat and Lisa got in the back. Reggie and Jay had been best friends since grade school and when Jay started dating his girlfriend Lisa in the first year of High school the three quickly became **inseparable**. Reg couldn't think of anyone else he would want to share his first drive of freedom with more.

"Do either of you know what the drive-in movie is tonight?" Reggie asked.

"Haha you were the one who planned it Reg, all you told us was to bring the snacks" Laughed Lisa as she opened her bag revealing a treasure of chocolate, candy and soda. "All we need to round this off is some popcorn and we're set!" she added "but keep your eyes on the road, not the sweets driver."

Dusk was already turning to night as Reggie drove, the gang of friends singing along to the radio whenever a song they liked began to play, none of them able to hold a tune but having fun anyway. It was past 8 and already dark when they arrived at the drive-in, a cold October night's clouds masking the moon and making it even darker than normal, the perfect conditions for a scary movie night.

"I'll grab the popcorn guys, Reg you sort out the microphone" said Jay as he hopped out the front seat and made his way to the concession stand. Reg knew Jay was very particular about his popcorn and whatever he bought back would be more butter than popcorn but he didn't mind. The night was going smoothly and apart from a little trouble with the taught elastic cable connecting the speaker to its power source straining against the car door everything was fine, Reggie could move the car forward to give the cord some slack but was nervous about being so close to another car. Who knew who's door may fly open and dent the side of his dad's precious car? His father's words of warning haunting him almost as much as he was sure the movie would.

Jay returned with the popcorn and it was about as buttery as Reggie had expected, the gang settled in as the movie began, the title reading 'VAMPIRE ZOMBIES FROM PLANET Z!' 'I guess I was right about the movie either way.' Reggie thought as they watched the movie on the big screen. It was of the silliest attempts at horror they'd ever seen, they found themselves laughing at the special effects more than gasping at the frights though friends had a great time anyway. The evening was so entertaining that once the credits began to roll Reggie, distracted by the night's excitement and his tight curfew, forgot to disconnect the speaker as he reversed the car out of its space; he was too eager to beat the traffic and make it home in time. PING, with a shocking snap the speaker whipped out of the car barely missing Reggie as it flew out the window and right into the driver's side wing mirror with a harsh crack! 'Oh Nooo' Reggie let out a low moan as he looked at the broken mirror, his friends gasped in shock, he wanted to scream and shout but he collected himself. Reggie grabbed the broken mirror and began the drive home, he knew he had to get his friends home otherwise they'd all be in trouble for breaking curfew.

The drive home was much less happy than the drive to the movie. Once Jay and Lisa had done their best to comfort their best friend a tense silence had filled the car, not abating till they had reached the drop-off point and exchanged stilted goodbyes. Reggie's long drive home knotted his stomach with worry, he'd made a promise and broken it. What would his parents do? He'd never see his friends outside of school again! He solemnly trudged up the path home after parking the car in the driveway, wondering what to say. Before he had even reached the door his Dad had already appeared, clearly eager to check in on his son.

"Reggie home before curfew, good job! How was the film?" his father said. Reggie struggled to look his dad in the eyes, but he told him how his carelessness had caused his fathers prized vehicle damage and apologized, tears forming in his eyes as he expected his father to shout and ground him. But when no shouting began Reggie became confused, he looked up and was surprised by what he saw. He could see a soft smile on his father's face.

"Son, you weren't acting recklessly, you made an honest mistake and told me as soon as you could, you followed my instructions and displayed **integrity** by telling me straight away. I'm proud of you." Said his father warmly. Reggie was shocked!

"So I'm not grounded?" he asked, his mood starting to lighten.

"No, but tomorrow we're grabbing a replacement using your allowance and I'm going to show you how to replace the wing mirror." Reggie's dad smiled as he continued "But you can bet you're not driving my baby for the rest of the year."

Reggie laughed for the first time since the film, it seemed fair after all and he could feel his dad's pride in his honesty, he welcomed his dad's arm around his shoulder as they went inside for the night happy that overall, he'd had a good Halloween, even if the movie wasn't the biggest fright of the night.

SUMMARY

Reggie has just acquired his full driver's license and to celebrate he goes to see a horror movie at the drive in with his friends. Before leaving he is warned by his father to not let any damage happen to the car or he will be in trouble so he becomes very panicked when an accident occurs and results in damage to the car. Reggie drops off his friends after a tense ride home. Once home he immediately confesses what happened to his Father, but rather than being punished like he expected his father understands it was an accident and instead tells him he will teach him to maintain the car.

Reggie acaba de obtener su licencia de conducir, y para celebrarlo, va a ver una película de terror en el autocine con sus amigos. Antes de irse, su padre le advierte que no permita que le ocurra ningún daño al automóvil o se meterá en problemas, por lo que entra en pánico cuando sucede un accidente y resulta en daños al automóvil. Reggie deja a sus amigos después de un viaje tenso a casa. Una vez en casa, inmediatamente confiesa lo que le sucedió a su padre, pero en lugar de ser castigado como esperaba, su padre entiende que fue un accidente y le dice que le enseñará a mantener el auto.

VOCABULARY

Relented: Ser menos severo o intenso.

Integrity: La cualidad de ser honesto y tener fuertes principios morales; rectitud moral.

Inseparable: No se puede separar o tratar por separado.

Determined: Haber tomado una decisión firme y estar resuelto a no cambiarla.

Organize: Hacer arreglos o preparativos para un evento o actividad; coordinar.

QUESTIONS

1. Where are the group headed?

A) Drive-In.

B) Drive-Thru.

C) Trick or treating.

D) To a party.

E) To the theater.

2. Who gets the popcorn?

A) Reggie.

B) James.

C) Tony.

D) Jay.

E) Neil.

3. When did Reggie get his license?

A) 2 months ago.

B) 1 month ago.

C) 2 weeks ago.

D) 1 week ago.

E) It doesn't say.

4. How much time was Reggie hoping to arrive home before curfew?

A) 10 minutes.

B) 15 minutes.

C) 20 minutes.

D) 25 minutes.

E) 30 minutes.

5. What holiday is it?

A) 4th of July.

B) Christmas.

C) Halloween.

D) Thanksgiving.

E) Winter Solstice.

Mummy Museum

The old museum on the hill was Wendy's favorite place in her city. It stood at the center of the city's main park on a hill, like a castle surrounded by green fields. Its large marble columns at the entrance made it look like a Greek temple or some sort of ancient palace, Wendy always thought it looked like it should be an exhibit itself! Ever since she had gone on a 8th grade field trip three years ago she wanted to work there and had been back every summer, the large entrance with its old ticket booth leading to an enormous central room that took her breath away with its grand structure every time she entered. On either side of the large room a large staircase led up to all three floors, each side of the floors dedicated to a different **aspect** of local and global history.

Wendy made a donation as she entered, as a citizen of the city she didn't have to pay but liked to support the museum anyway, feeling a sense of pride as she did. She paused for a moment to take a deep breath. One of the perks of the museum was the cold breeze of air conditioning in the summer, a luxury her own family's house did not have. Today she did not go right or left to the grand staircases as she usually would but instead began walking forward to the next room, its large double doors framed with swirling patterns of marble and gold. There would be plenty of time for the classic permanent exhibits but the main room beyond the atrium housed the more temporary exhibits and today was special, the main hall was entirely dedicated to Ancient Egypt! An Egyptian museum in Cairo had graciously accepted a cultural exchange and Wendy's local museum had donated suits of armor, pieces of castles and other local history. The Egyptian museum had donated many ancient relics as well including a Mummified Pharaoh!

Wendy could feel her excitement build as she entered the **exhibition** room, already a crowd had filled it. Wendy looked at the huge group of people, she had arrived early but clearly the excitement was not just hers! Moving through the crowd she began to look at the wonders of history before her. The idea of a civilization thousands of years older than hers was fascinating to young Wendy, a span of almost 5 thousand years between her and the creation of the ancient pieces of pottery now in front of her. She had read about how ancient Egyptians would make boats out of reeds which they would use to move goods between all the cities along the Nile in pots like this. The Nile itself was incredible to learn about, how its waters created rich soil on its banks, feeding most of Egypt and how in turn the Egyptians worshiped and understood it, their society tied to the Niles ebbs and flows.

Something beyond the small shards of pottery and the Nile exhibit caught Wendy's eye though and she made her way towards it. It was a small statue shaped like a cat. Wendy read the inscription underneath and was shocked to learn that an entire mummified cat was inside it! She had heard these stories before of Pharaohs and commoner's alike being buried with their pets out of love and respect, she had even heard that cats commanded such a high amount of respect in Egyptian society that they were almost considered gods! She walked past rows of funeral urns, each one inscribed with ancient hieroglyphs and shaped like the animal they contained, dozens of them lining the wall of the exhibition room. It wasn't long before Wendy reached the end of the urns, their placement designed to draw visitors to the main exhibit before her. It was a special room with a line in front, this was where they stored the Mummy! Wendy quickly lined up, hopping up and down with excitement. She had read the pamphlet before coming to the museum today and it had said that the mummies had to be kept in a special temperature controlled dark room to prevent damage from the light and the environment affecting them. The line moved at a brisk pace, encouraged by Museum staff and security along the way, Wendy was so filled with **anticipation** by the time she had reached the entrance she felt she could burst!

Entering the room Wendy had to take a minute to let her eyes adjust to the dark. As she did she could feel the change in the air, it was cool and dry unlike the humidity outside the museum. Her eyes could make out the outline of a glass covered platform in the center of the room, it was surrounded by **bollards** to help maintain a certain amount of distance between the Museum patrons and the Mummy. The crowd around it seemed almost respectfully silent as Wendy approached, muffled whispers being the loudest anyone seemed to talk. Wendy was awed by what she saw, before her was a beautiful golden coffin, she knew the ancient Egyptians called them sarcophagus's and they were reserved for only the most important people of their society. Even in the dim light the gold of the sarcophagus gleamed, its top in the shape of a man with a gorgeous head dress, the gems **inlaid** into it twinkling in the room's low light. Wendy could barely move; she was so entranced, knowing an ancient king laid within. How desperately she wanted to be someone who found such ancient and wondrous things, if she had any doubts about her future career they disappeared in that room.

Upon leaving Wendy almost felt in a daze, nothing could compare to what she saw. She had a small lunch at the museum cafe before checking all the old exhibits but could not get Egypt off of her mind, what a wondrous place. She let her mind wander and imagined becoming a world famous explorer, the next person to find an ancient pyramid or some lost relic of the past to show the world. She left the museum that day excited, knowing that it wasn't her dream anymore to work in the museum, but to be an archeologist.

SUMMARY

Wendy is a passionate student of history with aspirations of working in the local museum. She is excited to see a new exhibit the museum is hosting of ancient relics from Egypt. Once inside she spends her time looking over the artifacts, fascinated by Egyptian history and culture. Eventually Wendy makes her way to the room containing the mummified remains of a pharaoh and is overwhelmed with a desire to unearth more ancient pieces of history. Wendy leaves the museum no longer desiring to work there but instead to be an Archeologist.

Wendy es una apasionada estudiante de historia con aspiraciones de trabajar en el museo local. Está emocionada de ver una nueva exhibición que el museo presenta de reliquias antiguas de Egipto. Una vez dentro, pasa su tiempo mirando los artefactos, fascinada por la historia y la cultura egipcia. Eventualmente, Wendy se dirige a la habitación que contiene los restos momificados de un faraón y se siente abrumada por el deseo de desenterrar más piezas antiguas de la historia. Wendy deja el museo sin desear trabajar allí, sino ser arqueóloga.

VOCABULARY

Aspect: Una parte particular o característica de algo.

Inlaid: Ornamentada con piezas incrustadas de un material decorativo a ras de la superficie.

Bollard: Una franja corta utilizada para desviar el tráfico de personas de un área.

Anticipation: La acción de esperar con entusiasmo algo.

Exhibition: Una exhibición pública de obras de arte o artículos de interés, que se lleva a cabo en una galería de arte o museo o en una feria comercial.

QUESTIONS

1. At the start of the story what does Wendy want to be?

A) An Archeologist.

B) Museum staff.

C) An Explorer.

D) A Chef.

E) It doesn't say.

2. Where is the exhibit?

A) To the left.

B) To the right.

C) Upstairs.

D) Downstairs.

E) Beyond the atrium.

3. What does the Museum donate to Egypt?

A) Guns.

B) Suits of armor.

C) Swords.

D) Books.

E) Pictures.

4. How much does Wendy pay to enter?

A) 1 Dollar.

B) 2 Dollars.

C) 3 Dollars.

D) It's free entry.

E) It doesn't say.

5. What animal urn does Wendy examine?

A) A Dog.

B) A Cat.

C) A Mouse.

D) A Rat.

E) A Crocodile.

My Day at the Farm

The road kicked up dust like a brown storm cloud either side of the car as my Pop and I drove down it, bouncing up and down as our SUV hit potholes and ruts, far from the smooth highway driving we had experienced only minutes before.

"Pop, do I have to stay with Uncle Harry and his kids this weekend?" I asked, pleading my case for the last time. "The countryside makes me itchy and we're hours away from anything." I said, stressing the 'any' in anything. "What about Aunty Judith, all she has to worry about are her cats." I continued. "Kimberly, we've discussed this. I won't hear it again; my brother's farm is on the way to your grandma and I'm going to be busy all weekend helping her move." My father's voice was gentle and understanding but also firm, I knew this was the end of the conversation. "Besides" he continued "I grew up here and it's a lovely place, it'll be good for you to see what your family built when we first moved to America."

 I looked away and rolled my eyes. I'd heard the story of our family's journey at least one hundred times, every Thanksgiving, Birthday, Christmas and even one particularly long wedding anniversary. I was already well trained in blocking it out, barely hearing the words like 'hardship' and **'perseverance'** as we pulled up to the simple house at the end of the long dirt road, its occupants already coming out the door to greet us, a large shadow and two smaller ones in the shade of the porch.

Pop left the car first, I admittedly dragged my feet when it came time to get out of the passenger seat, like if I was slow enough it would already be time to go by the time my feet hit the ground. I came around the car in time to see my uncle embrace my Pop like he hadn't seen him in years.

"It's been too long brother" my uncle's deep voice boomed.

"Dad, we saw Uncle Evan and Kimberly just over a month ago." The gentle voice of my cousin Robert teased my uncle as he stepped into view from the shaded porch, him and his younger sister Poppy descending the step from the porch to the driveway. It was true, the last time we saw each other was in the garage of our Aunt Rosalina's house as our parents danced and sang inside, it wasn't awkward, but we didn't know each other that well. We all said our hellos as Uncle Harry helped me with my bags and I said goodbye to Pop.

"don't worry lil' Kimmy I'll be back before you know it" he said using our nickname for me as he hugged me close before getting back in the car and turning back to me. "Behave for your uncle till I get back" he said and with that he was gone, our SUV once again kicking up a dust cloud along the drive.

I watched the car's dust cloud as it drove down the road till it began to settle. Then I went to go help my uncle with my bags but before I even got close he politely shooed me away.

"Aww bless ya Kimberly, my brother raised a good girl but I've got this you run along with your cousins" I smiled and complied, liking this idea much more than lugging my bags up a flight of stairs plus while I wasn't a fan of the farm I did like my cousins, they always made me laugh.

"Long time no see cousin" Poppy said teasingly and with a sly wink "I know you're not exactly a country girl but we can still show you a fun time around here, c'mon" Poppy continued with a wave of her arm and the three of us set off to the fields near the house, as we reached the first field behind the house I could see the familiar boxy shapes of uncle Harry's prize dairy cows, big **lumbering** beasts with more in common with a Labrador dog in terms of attitude than what I thought of as a dumb barn animal. As we approached the half a dozen or so cows they moved to the edge of the fence eager for some attention. "Their coats remind me of Dalmatian's" I mentioned as we approached, taking in their black and white coats that almost shone with the warm light of the sun.

"Do you think they're black with white spots or white with black spots" Robert asked jokingly.

 "I didn't realize you became such a philosopher since the last time I'd seen you cousin." I said with a smile. Eager moos from across the fence helped put my mind at ease as I began my attempt to cross the fence, holding my breath as I stepped on the rickety stools that helped us hop the electric fence.

"Don't get distracted Kim, these big ol' girls will be here when we get back, our new friends are in the next paddock over" Poppy said, helping me get my legs across the fence without issue "but be careful where you step on the way, dads made sure they eat well" I laughed and made a note to watch my footing, I wouldn't be stepping in any cow pies today.

It wasn't far to the next fence, maybe only 10 minutes but I could hear the **commotion** beyond it before I saw anything, it was some of the loudest, most nerve **wracking** grunts and squeals that I'd ever heard. 'Why did dad leave me here, it sounds like they made a monster since the last time I was here' I thought to myself but my cousins beckoned me along and I followed hesitantly.

"What's beyond that fence it sounds scary" I asked Poppy, no longer able to contain my curiosity.

"Dad got some new pigs allllll the way from a place called 'New Zealand', says they'll win him big prizes at the next fair" Poppy replied, "I think they're called Kune Kune or something"

 "Koo-neigh Koo-neigh?" I responded by sounding out the strange words. 'Well okay pigs can't be that bad' I thought to myself, "soft and pink with curly tails I could handle that' I quickly found out how incorrect my assumptions were. We had reached the fence gate and the source of the commotion; these were no ordinary pigs! I almost ran when I saw their size, they almost rivaled the cows! With coarse brown fur, a big forehead ridge and tusks the size of my arm these were pigs that looked more like cavemen!

"Don't be afraid Kim" Robert said smiling "I know they look scary but they're the sweetest animals you've ever met" He ushered me to the enclosure and showed me how to pet one. "They're scary at first but they have more in common with teddy bears then wild boars" He laughed and the one closest to me gave my arm a big **slobbery** lick.

"See they like you, by the end of the weekend you'll even be able to ride one" Poppy said, tussling the fur on top of another's head.

"You can do that?" I exclaimed with shock.

"Only one way to find out cuz" Replied Poppy and her and her brother laughed.

"C'mon that's enough excitement for the day, Dad should be starting dinner soon let's get back to the house" Robert said shooing the large creatures away "there will be plenty of time to get to know our new friends tomorrow."

As we made our way back to the farmhouse I had to admit, I had a weekend ahead with a fun family and strange new creatures to play with, maybe farm life wasn't so bad after all, I might even enjoy it if I gave it a chance. I smiled to myself, Pop was right this was going to be a great weekend.

SUMMARY

Kimberly is upset she has to spend the weekend with her family at the farm while her dad helps her Grandmother move. After pleading with her father to no avail they arrive and Kimberly proceeds to spend time with her cousins. They enjoy each other's company while navigating electric fences and other hazards until they come across Kimberly's Uncle's newest addition to the farm, some exotic pigs. While initially scared, Kimberly comes to appreciate the sweet animals and decides that her time at the farm may not be so bad with such interesting animals and fun family to spend time with.

Kimberly está molesta porque tiene que pasar el fin de semana con su familia en la granja mientras su papá ayuda a su abuela a mudarse. Después de suplicarle a su padre en vano, llegan y Kimberly procede a pasar tiempo con sus primos. Disfrutan de la compañía del otro mientras navegan cercas eléctricas y otros peligros hasta que se encuentran con la última incorporación del tío de Kimberly a la granja, unos cerdos exóticos. Aunque inicialmente asustada, Kimberly llega a apreciar a los dulces animales y decide que su tiempo en la granja puede no ser tan malo con animales tan interesantes y una familia divertida con la que pasar el tiempo.

VOCABULARY

Lumbering: Moverse de una manera lenta, pesada e incómoda.

Wracking: Sujeto a estrés extremo.

Slobbery: Húmedo y viscoso.

Commotion: Un estado de perturbación confusa y ruidosa.

Perseverance: Persistencia en hacer algo a pesar de la dificultad.

QUESTIONS

1. Where is Kimberly's father going?

A) On holiday.

B) To work.

C) Overseas.

D) To help a family member.

E) Camping.

2. Who owns the farm?

A) Kim's Grandad.

B) Kim's Cousin.

C) Kim's Father.

D) Kim's Uncle.

E) Kim's Aunt.

3. When is Kimberly's dad coming back?

A) In a day.

B) 2 days.

C) In a week.

D) At the end of the weekend.

E) It's not clear.

4. How many pigs are in the pen?

A) 3.

B) 4.

C) 5.

D) 6.

E) It doesn't say.

5. What do the cows remind Kimberly of?

A) Dogs.

B) Bulls.

C) Pigs.

D) Cats.

E) Goats.

Rainbow Land

Sam was excited, he had never been to Rainbow Land but finally his school was taking him. Every year his school took the dozen students who had shown the best behavior to the theme park as a reward. Normally Sam's family couldn't afford such an expense but the school had a generous discount with the park, this along with Sam saving all his pocket money for the year meant he was able to go with his parents blessing.

The bus had picked him and his classmates early from outside the school and after a forty minute drive Sam could already begin to see the familiar outline of Rainbow Land near the highway exit. Its roller coaster and drop towers creating an unmistakable view, it almost felt like an unbelievable **mirage** Sam had been waiting for so long for this day. The bus hummed with excitement as the other students noticed the theme park and started to **chatter** amongst themselves, each talking about the rides they wanted to go on first.

"I want to try the haunted house." Said a girl with glasses who Sam didn't recognize.

"I want to go on the pirate ship first." Said another boy. It seemed the class couldn't agree where to go first and soon the bus was filled with arguments and heated discussion.

"Alright calm down now students." A large masculine voice rose above the noise of the students, punctuating his sentence with a booming clap you could hear all the way In the back of the bus, even over the student's voices. It was Mr. Douglas the school gym teacher and main chaperone of the trip.

"Now I know you are all very excited but I still want you to be on your best behavior" Mr. Douglas continued, "Once we're inside we will be with another group from MacCready Intermediate, be good and we will be able to see everything today alright class?"

"Yes Mr. Douglas." Sam and his fellow student replied in unison, no one wanted to risk not getting to enjoy the day they had waited so long for.

The bus pulled into Rainbowlands' large parking lot and each student thanked the driver as they disembarked before forming a line to go through the ticket booth. Mr. Douglas led his column of students, each one practicing an almost military level of focus in their formation as they marched into the park to meet with the other school. No one wanted to risk Mr. Douglas's attention and being sent back to the bus for misbehavior. The class met with their counterparts from the other school in the main plaza just beyond the entrance, brief introductions were made by Mr. Douglas and his fellow chaperone, a younger woman with kind eyes but clearly a fellow teacher named Miss Hitchens. After introductions were made the teachers turned their attention to the combined group.

"Now as you all know Rainbowland very generously allows us a discount for this yearly event and in return we can't have any of you running off it would get us in a lot of trouble understood?" Said Miss Hitchens and the group responded in the affirmative, ready to get the show on the road and see the theme park.

The groups adventure through Rainbowland began without an issue, some of the students taking interest in the smaller rides in the main plaza such as the carousel which chimed with sweet and gentle music as its plastic horses bobbed up and down or the carnival games with their tempting offers of prizes for a well thrown dart or skill with a pellet gun. But these small rides were not the ones Sam desired, he adored roller coasters even though they had never been on one, watching many videos on his phone of them and even having posters on their wall of some of the more famous ones. He knew from asking previous theme park trips students that it would be close to the end of the day when they went on the roller coaster but he could barely contain his excitement.

The day flew past with adventure and excitement, the terror of the haunted house turning into high speed action at the bumper cars and the gut churning momentum of the swinging pirate ship, a huge vessel that rocked back and forth like it was in a raging storm. But there was one ride Sam would not go on called 'The Meteor drop'. It was a huge tower that slowly rose to the top giving a perfect view of the park before free falling down to the bottom again, Sam hated heights so politely declined as they continued the day.

But the day took a turn after the pirate ship when Sam felt the need to use the washroom, he let his classmate know he'd be right back but when he left the bathroom he saw that the class had moved on without him! Sam wasn't sure what ride they would go on next and was desperate to find out where they could have gone before Mr. Douglas realized he wasn't with the group, thinking that he would send Sam back to the bus for getting lost!

Thinking fast there was one thing Sam knew he could do to find his group, only one place had a perfect view of the park: The Meteor Tower! With a gulp Sam swallowed his fear and got in line for the tower, it didn't take long for him to reach the front and he was quickly strapped into a harness with a group of tourists before the tower's lift began to **ascend**. Sam wanted to close his eyes but he knew this was his best chance to see where his group had gone so he **conquered** his nerves and kept his eyes open. The view was incredible as the lift rose higher and higher, Rainbowland stretched before him in every direction in an incredible view of theme park rides and flashing lights. But Sam wouldn't let himself get distracted, he **scanned** the paths and avenues of the park before seeing the familiar blue of his friends' school uniforms headed straight towards the roller coaster! Sam had just enough time to realize where his group was before he felt his stomach jump and the lift sent him flying down to the ground! Sam barely had time to soothe his frayed nerves from the sudden drop, he dismounted the ride and ran to his group, barely making it in time before the head count for the next ride!

Sam was overjoyed that he found his class and finally got to experience the excitement of a roller coaster, as the day came to an end and he got back on the bus all the children began to discuss their favorite rides.

Sam wondered, while he got a real kick out of finally getting to ride a real roller coaster, he couldn't stop thinking of the terror and excitement of The Meteor Drop, maybe it was his favorite ride of all!

SUMMARY

Sam is part of a field trip to the theme park Rainbow Land. He is very excited to go on a roller coaster for the first time but finds out that they won't be till the end of the trip. After meeting the other class on the field trip they proceed to enjoy the rides but Sam chooses not to go on a large tower called 'The Meteor Drop'. After becoming separated from the group Sam chooses to conquer his fears and go on 'The Meteor Drop' to see if he can see the group from a great height. Sam Succeeds in his endeavor and conquers his fears in time to ride the roller coaster. At the end of the day Sam reflects and decides after dealing with his fear that he may have enjoyed 'The Meteor Drop' more than the roller coaster.

Sam forma parte de una excursión al parque temático Rainbowland. Está muy emocionado de subirse a una montaña rusa por primera vez, pero descubre que no lo harán hasta el final del viaje. Después de conocer a la otra clase en la excursión, proceden a disfrutar de los paseos, pero Sam elige no subir a una gran torre llamada 'The Meteor Drop'. Después de separarse del grupo, Sam elige conquistar sus miedos e ir a 'The Meteor Drop' para ver si puede ver al grupo desde una gran altura. Sam tiene éxito en su esfuerzo y conquista sus miedos a tiempo para subirse a la montaña rusa. Al final del día, Sam reflexiona y decide después de lidiar con su miedo de que pudo haber disfrutado más de 'The Meteor Drop' que de la montaña rusa.

VOCABULARY

Mirage: Espejismo.

Chatter: Hablar rápido.

Ascend: Moverse, trepar o ir hacia arriba; montar; subir.

Scanned: Mire todas las partes de algo cuidadosamente.

Conquered: Ganar, ganar u obtener por esfuerzo.

QUESTIONS

1. What is the theme park's name?

A) Land of Rainbows.

B) Rainbowland.

C) Rainbow Land.

D) Rainbow's End.

E) Fun park.

2. What is the name of the second teacher?

A) Mr. Douglas.

B) Mr. Hitchens.

C) Miss Douglas.

D) Miss Hitchens.

E) Miss Hutchens.

3. What ride is Sam afraid of?

A) The Rollercoaster.

B) The Bumper Cars.

C) The Log Ride.

D) The Meteor Drop.

E) The Rocket.

4. What ride does Sam want to go on the most?

A) The Rollercoaster.

B) The Bumper Cars.

C) The Log Ride.

D) The Meteor Drop.

E) The Rocket.

5. What group of people does Sam get on 'The Meteor Drop' with?

A) Nuns.

B) School Children.

C) Visitors.

D) Tourists.

E) Kindergartners.

The Recital

Mary was not a girl who became nervous easily but tonight she could really feel it. It was the night of her school's musical **recital** and she was the star. The whole school knew that her skill at the violin was unmatched and her voice was beautiful, many of her teachers were her admirers and her biggest supporters, she was a favorite in every classroom, her presence was always appreciated by them. She had a voice that was heard all over the school, her voice was so clear and powerful that one might hear the sound of her singing on a quiet day all the way at the football pitches on the other side of the school!

But she didn't feel that way today, not at all. She felt a huge knot in her stomach, she felt like someone had filled her shoes with cement and she could hardly stop sweating. Mary had never performed for a crowd this size, and especially not for all of her **peers**. Usually Mary played or sang for her small, elite music class and teachers or for her family at home but tonight it felt like the entire school had filled the auditorium for the recital.

Nervously peering from behind the curtain Mary could see the rows of teachers fill the first two rows. Her eyes focused on the stern principal of Castille Academy, Miss Javert sitting with her usual rigid authority in the first row. Behind the Principal and head Teachers she could see classes of her peers filling out the rows into the darkness in the back of the auditorium. Straining her eyes she tried to make out where any of her friends were in the crowd but the darkness gave nothing away.

Meanwhile behind the curtain it was organized chaos. Stage hands ferried performers to their marks and made last minute adjustments to lights and dials that Mary did not understand, but seeing the **haste** with which they moved she assumed they were important. Focusing on the backstage helped, she could distract herself by watching others prepare, she tried not to wonder if they were as nervous as her. She made eye contact with the music teacher Miss Stevens as she was talking to the opening act, Miss Stevens glanced up and gave her a big smile and an encouraging thumbs up. Mary returned the gesture with her own thumbs up but felt it to be slightly less than convincing, she hoped Miss Stevens hadn't noticed.

Suddenly she could hear a hush fall over the crowd and she could tell from the light slipping from beneath the curtain starting to fade that everyone had found their seats, the show was about to begin! Mary had to remind herself to breathe, she still had time she wasn't on till well over halfway through the show. The first group of her peers took the stage, a dance troupe from the year below her. Mary took a position at the side of the stage and watched their entrance. Each dancer seemed to move with a free spirited grace as they entered the stage, all their outfits clashing with bright colors. But each one moved with perfect coordination with the others, the outfits begin to blend in a dazzling display of athletics. She remembered seeing them practice in the hall weeks before as she prepared her violin solo. Mary recalled how they had drilled themselves constantly, every time they fell or missed a step they stopped and started again. Over and over and over she had watched them practice, admiring their drive and passion that they would never seem to be upset by their mistakes, only seeking to improve.

It was the same with the next act, the school's band of which her friend Poppy was a part. She had remembered when Poppy had first begun drumming a year ago and how shy she was to perform in front of others but here she was performing with enthusiasm in front of the entire school. Her drumming provided the tempo and rhythm for the entire band. Mary had to stop from cheering too loudly when her friend launched into a smooth drum solo in the middle of the act, her friends in the band filling in perfectly once more when she was done.

Mary was so enraptured by her friend's performance that she had almost ignored her call up, the stage hand grabbed her shoulder lightly, tugging it to let her know she'd be next up.

Mary closed her eyes and swallowed her fears, this was it, it was time to show everybody what she had been practicing. Poppy hugged Mary as she and her band left the stage, Poppy was giggling and full of **adrenaline**.

"I can't wait to see you perform Mary." she said, breaking the hug and heading back stage, leaving Mary alone at the edge of the stage. Mary took a deep breath before stepping over the threshold and into the view of the crowd, there would be no turning back now she thought. Mary began as she had rehearsed, launching into a soft and sad opera solo, her voice starting small before growing to fill the entire auditorium. It was like clockwork, she thought. Her hours upon hours of practice had paid off and she could barely even notice the crowd as she began her routine. By the time she had finished her song and begun her violin solo she was completely in her element, it was like the crowd had melted away. She would glance at the crowd and only see smiles as they were entranced by her music. It was over before she knew it. Like she had left a **trance** once the last note was played and with a short bow the crowd erupted into applause, it'd felt like no time at all had passed since she had stepped onto the stage. Mary could already barely remember the pit in her stomach the nerves had created, her hard work is what mattered and it showed. Her skill was apparent and instead her stomach felt like it was full of butterflies of joy as she made her way back to the stage and to the cheers of Poppy and the rest of her friends.

SUMMARY

Mary is a gifted violin player and opera singer. Today is the night of one of the largest school performances and she begins to feel the pressure mounting. She tries to calm down but finds little reassurance till the show starts. As she watches her friends and other performers play she remembers how their hard work and hours of practice, failure and uncertainty has paid off and they all put on magnificent shows. Encouraged by this Mary takes the stage and sings, finding that after all of her own practice the performance comes naturally and isn't scary at all, happy with her performance Mary goes back to rejoin the others in celebration

Mary es una talentosa violinista y cantante de ópera. Hoy es la noche de una de las representaciones escolares más grandes y comienza a sentir que la presión aumenta. Ella trata de calmarse, pero encuentra poca tranquilidad hasta que comienza el espectáculo. Mientras observa a sus amigos y otros artistas tocar, recuerda cómo su arduo trabajo y horas de práctica, el fracaso y la incertidumbre han valido la pena y todos han realizado espectáculos magníficos. Animada por esto, Mary sube al escenario y canta, descubriendo que después de toda su propia práctica, la actuación es natural y no asusta en absoluto, feliz con su actuación, Mary regresa para reunirse con los demás en la celebración.

VOCABULARY

Recital: Un programa o concierto de estudiantes de danza o música para demostrar sus logros o progreso.

Peers: Un compañero o camarada.

Haste: Rapidez de movimiento; velocidad.

Adrenaline: La sensación de excitación, alerta e intensidad.

Trance: Un estado de completa absorción mental o meditación profunda.

QUESTIONS

1. What instrument does Mary's friend play?

A) Violin.

B) Drums.

C) Guitar.

D) Bass.

E) Keyboard.

2. What is the Principal of the school's last name?

A) Steven.

B) Javier.

C) Javert.

D) Stevens.

E) Poppy.

3. What Instrument does Mary play?

A) Violin.

B) Drums.

C) Guitar.

D) Bass.

E) Keyboard.

4. Who HAS Mary played in front of before?

A) Her parents.

B) Her Church.

C) Her school.

D) Her friends.

E) No one.

5. When did Mary's friend first start playing her instrument?

A) 1 month ago.

B) 1 week ago.

C) 1 year ago.

D) 2 months ago.

E) 2 years ago.

Shooting Stars

"Do you really think there's no such thing as aliens Fred?"

It was the question asked to me by my best friend Annie, a **recurring** one almost every weekend since grade school.

"Not now Annie, I just arrived." I replied hoping to avoid the discussion tonight. It was the end of year party for our high school, a bonfire on the beach nearby and it was true, I had just arrived moments ago and taken a seat next to Annie and my other friends Dave and Michelle.

"Well too bad me and Dave had just been talking about it." Continued Annie. I rolled my eyes. I knew she had **press-ganged** Dave into the conversion, I shot him a glance and he looked at me apologetically.

"You know I don't Annie, we have the same debate every weekend. What makes you think tonight's going to be any different?" I responded wearily, I loved my best friend but sometimes her fixations could become an annoyance.

"How couldn't it be different? With all the UFO sightings across the state this week how could you not believe it?" Annie gestured to the sky as she talked, like a Flying saucer would come down and land on the beach as she spoke.

"It's shooting stars Annie, the weather guys predicted this weeks ago." I said, hoping it would be enough but knowing this wouldn't be enough to rest the debate for the night the party going on around us would have to wait.

"Actually it was **astrologists**." **Interjected** Michelle, "But I guess that's not really the point." she added.

"Either way, of course that's when the UFO's would show up." Annie continued, clearly undeterred by her disbelieving audience.

"It's the perfect cover to observe us more closely, I bet you those aren't all stars flying across our sky." Annie finished, with a dramatic look up that was only slightly ruined by the fact there were no stars shooting overhead yet tonight.

The conversation finally changed after some time and our group mingled with the party. It was good to celebrate the end of the year with our friends from school. Some of them were dancing on the beach to the tinny sound of a car radio nearby and others playing a game of football in the sand, though the dark of the night was making any competitive game difficult. But eventually as the night wore on I found myself sitting with Annie again, she had that familiar look in her eyes, I knew what was coming.

"Don't start please Annie." I said.

"Start what?" She replied with a smile.

"Talking about little green men in shiny spaceships, with tentacles and forked tongues, that stuff." I answered.

Annie pouted, "Now you know I don't think they look like that, all of UFO science agrees they're tall and gray with big spooky eyes... or lizardmen." she said, trailing off, maybe realizing how crazy some of what she said sounded. The debate continued in circles as usual, neither of us giving an inch, me the skeptic and Annie always somehow amazed by my skepticism.

"So you don't think that in our big and infinite universe that there are other beings like us?" Annie asked quizzically.

"I'm not saying that, what I'm saying is the odds of them coming all the way to Earth just to say hello to us during a meteor storm seem extremely unlikely." I said trying to **placate** my friends needs to be right.

"AHA" She exclaimed like she had won a major victory, and with a smile said "So you admit there's a chance?"

I sighed loudly, there would be no settling this debate tonight, Annie was firing on all cylinders.

It was then though that I started to hear gasps from the crowd, we looked around and could see people with their heads up, looking at the stars. Another meteor shower had begun and it was one of the most incredible ones I had ever seen. Quick streaks of light whizzed across the open night sky with such frequency and intensity it felt more like a blanket of light was streaking across the sky. Some stars had lighter or darker tails creating a fascinating criss cross pattern in the sky, streaks of orange and darker yellow intersecting with the brighter light of the other stars. I looked down momentarily at my friends, each one with eyes full of wonder. Regardless of what we believed was in the night sky that night I felt a warm feeling of love knowing I was here with all my friends sharing a beautiful and rare moment.

It was then that I looked up and out of the corner of my eye just above the treeline nearby one shooting star heading off in a direction unlike the rest. I focused my attention on it, its trail a light green instead of the other hues of yellow and it moved almost lazily and in a different direction to the rest. It was only for a moment and before my brain could even realize what I was seeing and tell the others it was gone. The storm of stars was dying down and the party began again in earnest, conversations picked up where they left off and dancing began once more. I wondered if I should tell my friends what I thought I saw, that maybe Annie wasn't entirely wrong, but what did I see? Maybe it was a trick of the light or a helicopter, maybe even a prank, I couldn't just go and assume it was green men from mars straight away could I? I decided to stay quiet for now and enjoy the night with my friends. But next time Annie brought up the conversation of aliens I considered having a more sympathetic ear, after all it was clear that there were more things in this world and in the sky than I could explain, who could say which one of us was right?

SUMMARY

Fred meets his friends at the end of the school year beach party. The group engage in a conversation that is recurring due to their alien obsessed friend Annie. The conversation goes back and forth, heightened by the meteor showers that have been happening recently. Eventually the group spend time enjoying the party before being distracted by another meteor shower. During the shower Fred notices a meteor acting strangely in a way he cannot explain, deciding not to tell the group but resolving to approach things with a more open mind in the future.

Fred se encuentra con sus amigos en la fiesta en la playa de fin de año escolar. El grupo entabla una conversación que es recurrente debido a su amiga Annie, obsesionada con los extraterrestres. La conversación va y viene, acentuada por las lluvias de meteoritos que han estado ocurriendo recientemente. Finalmente, el grupo pasa un tiempo disfrutando de la fiesta antes de distraerse con otra lluvia de meteoritos. Durante la lluvia, Fred nota que un meteorito actúa de manera extraña, de una manera que no puede explicar, y decide no decírselo al grupo, pero decide abordar las cosas con una mente más abierta en el futuro.

VOCABULARY

Recurring: Ocurriendo o apareciendo de nuevo.

Press-ganged: Obligar a alguien a hacer algo.

Astrologist: Una persona que usa la astrología para contarles a otros sobre su carácter o para predecir su futuro.

Placate: Apaciguar o pacificar, especialmente mediante concesiones o gestos conciliadores.

Interjected: Iterponer entre otras cosas.

QUESTIONS

1. Which friend is obsessed with aliens?

A) Fred.

B) Annie.

C) Michelle.

D) Dave.

E) Gary.

2. Who brings up astrologists?

A) Fred.

B) Annie.

C) Michelle.

D) Dave.

E) Gary.

3. What color does Annie think the aliens are?

A) Green.

B) Pink.

C) Grey.

D) Blue.

E) Red.

4. What are the other kids doing on the beach?

A) Dancing.

B) Playing football.

C) Making a fire.

D) Sunbathing.

E) Eating.

5. What color was the strange meteor?

A) Blue.

B) Purple.

C) Orange.

D) Yellow.

E) Green.

Stone Soup

There was nothing in this world Mani **adored** more than his grandmother's cooking. Ever since he was young he could remember **savoring** the idea of family Thanksgiving at his 'Avo's' house as his mother called it. She told him Avo was the name for Grandmother where they came from, a far off place called Portugal. Mani had never been to Portugal, he'd lived in America all his life and it seemed very far away, his Avo telling him it took them almost two weeks to get to America by boat and even then they still had to come all the way to Chicago where the family settled sixty years ago!

There was one thing that always confused Mani though and he was mulling it over on the drive to Avo's this thanksgiving. He sat in the back passenger seat as his parents drove, wondering why every time they arrived at Avo's house for Thanksgiving there would be a big pot with a stone in it by the front door? As each family member came in they placed a piece of food in the pot before greeting his Avo with a big hug and enjoyed a warm welcome into the family home, his parents would always give him an item to add to the pot upon entry as well, though they had never explained why. So it was as every Thanksgiving, Mani and his parents pulled into his grandmother's driveway and they gave him an item for the pot, a sprig of rosemary and a bay leaf.

"But why Papa?" asked Mani, no longer able to contain his curiosity.

"Ah you're old enough to appreciate the story Mani, ask your Avo when we get in, okay?" His father replied, patting him on the shoulder.

As usual Mani and his parents were the first to arrive, his parents prided themselves on their **punctuality**, Mani placed his herbs alongside his mother and fathers offering, a chorizo and potato before embracing his grandmother in a warm hug.

"My little Neto" she cried happily, squeezing him tight. Neto was Portuguese for grandson and what Mani's grandma loved to call him. "Though not so little anymore, how old are you now?" his grandma continued.

"Ten years old Avo. He replied, returning the hug.

Once greetings had been exchanged and his family began to get comfortable after the drive Mani returned to his grandmother.

"Avo, why do you have a pot and a stone by the door?" He asked. Mani's grandmother smiled "Oh how I love this story, come help your Avo in the kitchen and I'll tell you while we work" she said. Mani could not resist the offer, he could already smell the turkey cooking in the oven with his grandmother's spicy Peri-Peri baste. He would have been happy to help knowing he'd be the first to taste his grandmother's delicious cooking even without the promise of the story.

Mani eagerly began to cut some potatoes, waiting for his grandmother to start her story. He knew better than to pester her; she liked to begin her stories at her own pace. As they worked, magical delicious scents filled the air, and more of their family arrived with even more offerings for the stone pot. More herbs and potatoes, bowls of beans and bacon as well began to fill it.

"It happened many years ago, well before your great grandmother was born but in the same village in Portugal that she was raised." Began Mani's grandmother suddenly, he immediately listened with **rapt** attention as she continued. "A wandering monk visited, hungry from his long journey but the villagers had suffered a bad harvest and no one was willing to feed him from their small food supplies. The monk, being a smart man, knew what to do. He smiled and told the villagers that it would be fine, he'd make his own meal but they were all welcome to join him if they chose too."

Mani's curiosity peaked, how could this **starving** monk make his own meal? He waited for his grandma to continue.

"The monk drew some water from a well, put it in his cooking pot and made a small fire in the square. What got the attention of the villagers though was when the clever monk pulled a smooth stone out of his travelers pack and placed it into the simmering pot. This attracted a group of villagers, they asked the monk what he was doing and he told them he was making stone soup."

Mani was confused, was the stone the meal? He was about to ask before his Avo once again picked up the story.

"The villagers' curiosity got the better of them and they asked if they could try some, the monk said of course they could but if it wouldn't be too much trouble he asked for them to help with some extra ingredients in return so their meal could feed more people. The villagers agreed, some bringing rosemary, salt and bay leaves for flavor, others bringing chorizo or bacon to season the water further, finally others bringing potatoes and white beans to thicken the soup. Before long the town square was filled with the smell of delicious soup and many bowls were shared between the monk and the villagers, music and celebration filled the square. Without knowing it the monk had taught them all to share, while no villager had enough ingredients for soup all of them together had everything needed for a delicious meal. Before he set off to leave on his journey the next day, the monk took his stone and placed it back in his pack, the villagers asked why he wasn't going to eat it and the monk replied he'd be saving it for later, to flavor another soup."

Mani was confused, "so it was a trick Avo? Why do you do it now?"

Mani's grandmother laughed and patted her grandson on the head, "Maybe long ago it was a trick Mani but the villagers kept the tradition of stone soup alive, every season the villagers would meet in the square and add a ingredient to the pot, it means to come together as a community and a family."

Mani looked at the pot by the door, it had filled to the brim as grandma and he had cooked and he had to agree, it was nice to see his family come together in such a physical way. Grandma winked at Mani and leaned close as if to share a secret "but Mani, the difference between my soup and that one is I tell the family what to bring, now you know why your

Avo has the best stone soup." Together they laughed as the family arrived and filled the home. Mani savored the smells of thanksgiving and the idea of a delicious stone soup to come, but most of all enjoyed his family coming together as one.

SUMMARY

Mani goes with his parents to Thanksgiving at his Grandmother's house. Along the way he questions a strange tradition his family have where when they enter their grandmother's home they place a random ingredient into a pot with a stone by the door. His parents tell him to ask his grandma later which Mani does, she responds by getting him to help her cook the thanksgiving dinner while she recounts the tale. Mani's Grandmother tells him the story of a wandering monk who convinces a reluctant town to help him make a soup using only a stone; the fable teaches togetherness and coming together as a community. Mani, satisfied with this answer, enjoys how the pot symbolizes his family coming together on this day and the delicious soup they'll be sure to eat soon.

Mani va con sus padres al Día de Acción de Gracias en casa de su abuela. En el camino, cuestiona una extraña tradición que tiene su familia en la que cuando ingresan a la casa de su abuela, colocan un ingrediente al azar en una olla con una piedra junto a la puerta. Sus padres le dicen que le pregunte a su abuela más tarde, ella responde que él la ayude a cocinar la cena de acción de gracias mientras ella cuenta la historia. La abuela de Mani le cuenta la historia de un monje errante que convence a un pueblo reacio para que lo ayude a hacer una sopa usando solo una piedra, la fábula enseña la unión como comunidad. Mani satisfecho con esta respuesta disfruta de cómo la olla simboliza la reunión de su familia en este día y la deliciosa sopa que seguramente comerán pronto.

VOCABULARY

Adored: Gustar o admirar mucho.

Savoring: Degustar una buena comida o bebida y disfrutarla por completo.

Punctuality: Estricta observancia en el cumplimiento de los compromisos, puntualidad.

Rapt: Con mucha.

Starving: Sentir una fuerte necesidad o deseo.

QUESTIONS

1. What is the name Mani calls his Grandma?

A) Ava.

B) Avo.

C) Abuela.

D) Grannie.

E) Gran.

2. What is the name Grandma calls Mani?

A) Nino.

B) Neto.

C) Nephew.

D) Nero.

E) Nina.

3. Who visits the town in the story?

A) A Monk.

B) A Priest.

C) A Merchant.

D) A King.

E) A Sailor.

4. What holiday is the family celebrating?

A) Christmas.

B) Groundhog Day.

C) Thanksgiving.

D) New Years.

E) Hanukkah.

5. Where did Manis' family emigrate from?

A) Spain.

B) Mexico.

C) Portugal.

D) France.

E) Poland.

The Two Ollies

"You can't name the dog after yourself Oliver, it'll be confusing who will I be calling to dinner?"

Mom was exasperated I could tell by the way she spoke, but the moment Dad had come home with a dog in the backseat of his truck I knew his name was Oliver.

"I'm sorry mom but look at him he's clearly an Oliver." I said.

The small puppy looked up from my lap, his hazel eyes matching mine, he even wore my favorite color as his coat bright yellow, there was no question in my mind.

"Fine but I'm calling him Ollie, from now on in this house you're Oliver young man." Said Mom, finally seeing a way she could benefit from this.

"But Moooom, that's my nickname." I complained.

I knew Mom thought at 12 I had begun to be too old for nicknames and began to complain more but mom cut me off quickly.

"No if's, and's or but's mister, now go show Ollie around his new home"

That was that. The whole summer Ollie and I were **inseparable**, most of my friends were at summer camp but my family lived on the outskirts of town and there were plenty of chores I needed to do for my family around the property so I had to stay behind. But my new companion came with me everywhere and thanks to Ollie I didn't miss my friends much, he made sure I had the best summer of my life. I meant it when I said we were inseparable, if Dad needed help roofing, 'Ollie and Ollie' would be there as my father called us even if mom didn't approve. Ollie was happy to lay in the shade of the chimney while he watched us work. But by far what became our favorite activity was spending time by the old stream just beyond the paddock behind our house, the only issue was the ornery old cows that grazed in the paddock. Ollie was growing quickly from the small puppy that arrived at the house, he already came up to above my knee after only 3 weeks, but he was still no match for those cows. He would cower every time one of the grizzled old bovines came close and I'd have to carry him the rest of the way across the paddock, he was as yellow as his fur it turned out!

But his **demeanor** would always change the moment we got to the stream, it was the perfect place to spend the summer. The sun warmed the water just enough that it was always pleasant to jump in and just deep enough that if I really stretched my legs, I could touch the bottom and keep my head above water. We spent most of our time swimming and lazing around but the one game Ollie loved most of all was whenever I'd throw a branch as far as I could downstream and he'd race along the riverbank to catch it before the current swept it out of reach downstream. He wouldn't always be fast enough though and the first time he ran off after a branch and didn't come back after an hour I was **distraught**. I was almost in tears thinking he was lost until when he came back cheering me up with licks to the face.

The scariest part of the summer came one unsuspecting morning though. It seemed like any other, I helped Mom bring in the laundry and dad clean the garage before being given permission to take Ollie and go to the stream. We walked to the back paddock, I carried my cowardly companion across the field of cows even though they had by this point gotten so used to my new friend and didn't even bother to investigate him. Not that this convinced Ollie that he no longer needed to be carried before reaching the edge of the property before the stream. Ollie let out a happy bark as we set off down the hill to the stream, his tongue lolling to the side as he panted in the dry summer heat. He was surely as happy as I was to be in the broad shade of the willow trees near the stream. There had been heavy rains the last few days making both of us a bit stir crazy in the house and we were eager to blow off some steam. We were so excited I forgot to take into account the strong current now flowing through our normally peaceful hangout and while I noticed the current a little, I was a strong enough swimmer to pay it no particular mind. This changed once me and Ollie decided to play fetch, Ollie had bought me a branch. He was bright enough to ask for what he wanted in his own doggie way, he nuzzled my side and stood over me as I lay drying on the bank.

"Okay Ollie I'll play" I said rubbing the canary yellow fur on the top of his head. I hefted the branch, a long surprisingly straight willow that must have fallen during the storm and hurled it like a javelin towards the clear waters of the stream, penetrating it smoothly before popping up some ways ahead. I had impressed myself, it was an excellent throw.

"Go get it boy!' I hollered as Ollie gave chase. Ollie was already leaping into the water with practiced ease but my delight at watching my best friend pursue his target quickly changed to concern. I watched Ollie struggle against the current and I realized I'd misjudged the water and now he was being swept along! I gave chase along the side of the riverbank, clambering over tree roots and slipping over wet stones as I tried to keep an eye on Ollie, but it wasn't enough. We'd reached where the current became faster even on a good day and I was watching my only friend this summer disappear out of view! I had to think fast, Ollie was keeping his head above water easily but couldn't reach the sides of the stream. I could follow the water to where it eased into a small lake just two miles away and if I cut through the woods there the river instead made a lazy bend I could get there even faster!

I ran with speed I didn't even realize I had, getting whipped in the face with a branch more than once for my efforts but continuing on regardless to save my Ollie. I realized I was getting close to the river's outlet into the lake when I saw a familiar four-legged shape in the distance, Ollie must have already made it out! I shouted for joy as I approached but quickly realized my mistake, the startled figure thought was Ollie turned toward me, already growling and with menacing eyes, it wasn't Ollie it was a wild dog! I was petrified as the creature slowly paced towards me with a frightful look in its eyes. I couldn't move, I could only watch as the angry dog came closer! I closed my eyes, shivering with fright, still frozen with terror. But then as I assumed it was all over, I heard the crack of underbrush and another even fiercer growl announced itself matching the wild dogs. I opened my eyes and there he was! Ollie was between me and his wild counterpart, soaking wet, **hackles** raised and the willow stick in his mouth, he'd caught it after all! I gingerly took the stick from Ollie's mouth and **brandished** it at our foe, both of us making a loud mixture of barks and yells. The wild dog sensibly realized it wasn't worth fighting the both of us and turned tail and ran, Ollie had saved my life!

I took a knee and hugged my pet with glee.

"Gee boy I guess you aren't a coward after all, I can't wait to tell all my friends they'll love you!" I said hugging Ollie, his tail now wagging excitedly to see me again. With that we set off home, tired of adventure for one day. Two things happened after that day, the first being Ollie walking through that paddock of cows with his head held high, clearly no longer a coward and the second being he never swam in the stream again for the rest of the summer.

SUMMARY

Oliver's father comes home with a dog which Oliver quickly named after himself. They spend the summer on the family farm helping with chores and playing in the river, though it's shown that Ollie the dog is quite timid around other animals. One day after a few days of heavy rain the two Ollie's go down to the river but the dog Ollie gets swept up in the current. Human Ollie gives chase and takes a shortcut to reach the lake the river flows into. On the way he has an encounter with a feral dog, fearing the worst until his pet intervenes. The two Ollies reunited happily go home.

El padre de Oliver llega a casa con un perro al que Oliver nombró rápidamente como él mismo. Pasan el verano en la granja familiar ayudando con las tareas del hogar y jugando en el río, aunque se muestra que el perro Ollie es bastante tímido con otros animales. Un día, después de unos días de fuertes lluvias, los dos Ollie bajan al río, pero la corriente arrastra al perro Ollie. Ollie humano lo persigue y toma un atajo para llegar al lago en el que desemboca el río. En el camino tiene un encuentro con un perro salvaje, temiendo lo peor hasta que interviene su mascota. Los dos Ollies reunidos regresan felices a casa.

VOCABULARY

Inseparable: Incapaces de ser separados.

Demeanor: Conducta, comportamiento.

Distraught: Distraído; profundamente agitado.

Hackles: Los pelos en la parte posterior del cuello y la espalda de un perro, gato, etc., que se levantan cuando el animal está enojado o asustado.

Brandished: Sacudir o agitar, utilizar algo como arma.

QUESTIONS

1. What animal is Dog Ollie afraid of?

A) Pigs.

B) Cows.

C) Chickens.

D) Dogs.

E) Wolves.

2. What season is the story set?

A) Summer.

B) Winter.

C) Autumn.

D) Spring.

E) It doesn't say.

3. Why Isn't Human Ollie with his friends?

A) He's grounded.

B) They Moved.

C) They went to summer camp.

D) He doesn't have friends.

E) He's on holiday abroad.

4. What animal do they encounter in the woods?

A) Pigs.

B) Cows.

C) Chickens.

D) Dogs.

E) Wolves.

5. What color is Ollie's dog?

A) Brown.

B) Black.

C) White.

D) Yellow.

E) Red.

Zookeeping

It was a hot summer day, the sun was beating down on Louis but he barely noticed as he stood in a courtyard of his local zoo. It was his first day as a junior zookeeper, a program started by his highschool for senior students interested in a **career** in zookeeping or animal care in general. Louis felt full of pride in his new uniform he had received that morning at orientation. It was only a simple but rugged **khaki** shirt, shorts and hat combination but the feeling of pride that filled him made it feel like he was wearing a **tuxedo**. He was waiting in the courtyard outside the main staff building of the zoo for the zookeeper he was meant to shadow for the rest of the day. As he waited he busied his mind by watching the other staff of the zoo busy themselves to prepare for the opening which was less than an hour away. Kitchen staff rushed to and from the delivery area nearby to transport ingredients to the zoo restaurant, alongside them zookeepers were taking larger boxes of vegetables and meat to a different building which he presumed would be where it was prepared for the animals.

It wasn't long before an older woman wearing the same sort of uniform that Louis had left the staff building, after seeing Louis she cut across the courtyard over to him she extended a hand as she got close. Louis took her hand and shook it as she began to speak.

 "You must be Louis, it's a pleasure to meet you, your teacher had many good things to say about you." Said the woman as she firmly shook his hand. The woman's hand was rough, Louis could tell that she was a hard worker, she must be a veteran of the Zoo he thought as she continued.

"My name is Zoey, I'm a senior zookeeper of 15 years and I'll be your main liaison for today. I'll be giving you tasks and making sure you complete them, hopefully by the end of the day hopefully you'll have an idea of what it takes to be a zookeeper."

Louis felt nervous he knew he wanted to impress Zoey, she was everything he wanted to grow up to be ever since his first trip to the zoo as an eight year old. With a smile Zoey turned on her heel and began to walk towards a door next to the staff area, Louis rushed after her. Louis was led through corridor after corridor, it felt like a maze.

 'This must be the service passages of the zoo, how maintenance workers and zookeepers get around without dealing with the crowds.' He thought to himself as they traveled. The smell in the corridors was less than pleasant, like a barn full of animals but Louis was expecting this, wild animals of course do not care particularly how they smell! It must have only been a three minute walk before Zoey took him into a room. It seemed to be a closed off portion of one of the exhibits, where the animals would rest and feed away from visitors. Louis looked around, the floors were covered in dirty straw and mess, it was clearly time for some room service. Zoey turned to face Louis before speaking. "This is the Zebras den, they're currently out in their enclosure for the guests so that gives you plenty of time to clean their stable." Zoey gestured towards the broom, trash bags and fresh hay near the door, Louis was disappointed it wasn't a more exciting animal enclosure but he supposed it made sense to start him here.

 "I have some other tasks that need my attention, I'll be back in an hour Louis, that should be enough time for you to clean our guest's room." Zoey said with a wink before turning on her heel and headed out the way they had come. Like that Louis was alone, his first day as a Zookeeper truly began, it was glamorous but he knew he had an important job to do.

It wasn't an easy job cleaning out an animal pen but Louis approached it with a sense of professionalism, eager to create a good first impression. It was a messy and smelly job but Louis did it with a continued sense of pride like he had felt in the courtyard. He knew not every part of caring for animals professionally was fun or exciting but it was necessary to keep things clean for the animals, even if he had to hold his breath at points as he raked up the old hay.

Louis' hard work had paid off and he had finished his task with time to spare. He surveyed the animal pen with its fresh hay, clean floors and full food troughs and smiled. He was about to go look for another Zookeeper to let them know he had finished as Zoey entered the room suddenly. Her hat was slightly damaged on the top, as if claws had been raked across it. Zoey could see Louis' attention to it and began to speak.

"Don't worry just a little excitement in the Koala exhibit, sometimes they get a little rowdy and drop from the trees to surprise you, it's a perk of the job." she said and laughed, clearly unfazed. Zoey surveyed the room, nodding approvingly as she did.

"Good work Louis, very professional job, you worked on a farm before? Either way I think you earned a little reward for your grunt work." Zoey said, leading Louis to the door separating the pen and the exhibit before removing its dead bolt and letting it swing open, she walked out the door and gave a sharp long whistle. It wasn't long before Louis could see why, suddenly zebras began gently and cautiously entering the stable.

'The herd must be used to the whistle meaning lunchtime.' He thought. The zebras were bigger than he expected, he had never seen them up close and they were surprisingly bold, clearly used to the presence of Zookeepers. Zoey reached out to pet one's black and white mane as it walked past and encouraged Louis to do the same, he was **enthralled** by the creatures. Louis reached out and the Zebras mane felt tough and bristly in his hand almost like the head of a broom. He felt happy as he did so, his hard work had paid off and as he stood in the stable surrounded by wonderful exotic animals he knew for certain he had found his calling and was already looking forward to coming back the next day for more. "When do I get to meet the lions?" Louis asked Zoey.

She laughed before replying "Maybe after three to four years of work and an animal handling degree, then we can talk about it my eager young friend." They both laughed together but Louis was **undeterred**, if that's what it took he knew he would achieve it, his future was bright.

SUMMARY

It's Louis' first day as a junior Zookeeper and he is very excited. As he waits to meet his supervisor he appreciates his new uniform and the activity of other staff members around him. Eventually his trainer, a senior Zookeeper named Zoey arrives and takes him to his first job. They take a quick journey through the staff area of the zoo before Zoey leaves Louis in the Zebra stables and leaves him to clean it while she takes care of other jobs around the zoo. Louis does a good job and is rewarded with a chance to meet the Zebras, this strengthens his resolve to become a fulltime Zookeeper in the future.

Es el primer día de Louis como cuidador junior del zoológico y está muy emocionado. Mientras espera para encontrarse con su supervisor, aprecia su nuevo uniforme y la actividad de otros miembros del personal a su alrededor. Finalmente, su entrenadora, una cuidadora del zoológico de alto nivel llamada Zoey, llega y lo lleva a su primer trabajo. Hacen un viaje rápido a través del área de personal del zoológico antes de que Zoey deje a Louis en los establos de Zebra y lo deja para limpiarlo mientras ella se ocupa de otros trabajos en el zoológico. Louis hace un buen trabajo y es recompensado con la oportunidad de conocer a las cebras, lo que fortalece su decisión de convertirse en un cuidador del zoológico a tiempo completo en el futuro.

VOCABULARY

Career: Una ocupación o profesión, especialmente una que requiere entrenamiento especial.

Khaki: Tela gruesa de algodón trenzado de color marrón amarillento, que se usa especialmente para hacer uniformes.

Tuxedo: Chaqueta de hombre para traje de noche semi formal, tradicionalmente de color negro o azul oscuro.

Enthralled: Cautivado o encantado.

Undeterred: Sin inmutarse, sin desanimarse.

QUESTIONS

1. What is Louis' role?

A) Junior Zookeeper.

B) Zoo Keeper.

C) Zookeeper.

D) Senior Zookeeper.

E) Assistant Zookeeper.

2. What degree will Louis need in the future?

A) Animal Management.

B) Animal Handling.

C) Animal Charming.

D) Animal Husbandry.

E) Animal Care.

3. How long does he have to clean the animal pen?

A) 1 hour.

B) 30 minutes.

C) 15 minutes.

D) 1 hour and fifteen minutes?.

E) It doesn't say.

4. What animal damages Zoey's hat?

A) Koala.

B) Badger.

C) Horse.

D) Zebra.

E) Lion.

5. What Animal pen is Louis cleaning?

A) Koala.

B) Badger.

C) Horse.

D) Zebra.

E) Lion.

Answers

An Adventure in Teotihuacan

C,A,A,B,D

The Arcade

A,D,B,B,E

The Beautiful Game

C,B,A,C,D

The Colorful Water

B,D,C,A,E

Camp Green Lake

C,A,A,B,B

Camping

C,A,A,E,B

Doctor Visit

A,B,D,C,B

Grandma's Parakeet

E,C,A,B,E

Island Experience

B,D,C,A,E

Kim's Beach

B,C,D,E,A

Lost in New York

B,A,E,C,A

Movie Night

A,D,E,B,C

Mummy Museum

B,E,B,E,B

My Day at the farm

D,D,D,E,A

Rainbow Land

C,D,D,A,D

The Recital

B,C,A,A,C

Shooting Stars

B,C,C,B,E

Stone Soup

B,B,A,C,C

The Two Ollies

B,A,C,D,D

Zookeeping

A,B,A,A,D

¡No te olvides de descargar las historias traducidas!

Visita nuestro sitio web y descárgalas para seguir la lectura en paralelo.

https://acquirealot.com/translated-stories/

NOTES

A special request

Help us reach more people, your brief review could help us a lot!, please look in your recent orders for this book and leave your comments. Your support really does make a difference, we will read all the reviews one by one.

Thank you very much!

About the Author

Acquire a Lot is an organization dedicated to teaching languages effectively, based on an innovative method developed by teachers of the organization, called LRPR, that has the following fundamental pillars to ensure you can acquire the language naturally:

- Listen to stories
- Read stories
- Play games to solidify what you have learned
- Repeat

Acquire a Lot's mission is to encourage language acquisition instead of the traditional method. With the LRPR method, there are no grammar lessons, there are no corrections, and everything is acquired naturally, in the same way a child develops his/her first language.

For more information, you can visit our website:

www.acquirealot.com

Books in this Series

Books By This Author

available at
amazon

Printed in Great Britain
by Amazon